T0266665

KYOTO GARDENS

Masterworks of The Japanese Gardener's Art

Text by Judith Clancy

Photography by Ben Simmons

TUTTLE Publishing

Tokyo | Rutland, Vermont | Singapore

CONTENTS

Above Symbolic summer lotus.

Bottom from left A picturesque pose by the Zen garden at Kennin-ji. A single camellia leaf spout for a stone fountain at Honen-in. *Miko* shrine maiden serves tea at Jonan-gu Shrine. Swirling waves of gravel in the Yang Rock Garden at Taizo-in. A *maiko* apprentice geisha on an autumn outing at Kitano Tenmangu Shrine.

reshaping the land

Long ago, the shadow of a large pterosaur swept across a prehistoric land. Buffered by air currents, the winged predator surveyed the wave-trimmed coastlines and peaked ridges.

Today, it is the undulating shadow of an airplane that skims the same glistening peaks and white sand coasts. Forests of houses and factories have displaced dense woodlands, and rivers of asphalt cross ancient streams.

The Japanese archipelago stretches from the temperate island of Hokkaido with its long, snowy winters to the semitropical coral reef islands in the Okinawan chain. The country ranges from 45 to 26 degrees latitude, the distance from Milan to Dubai, from Montreal to Miami.

Front endpaper Bronze basin filled with fallen camellia flowers from the garden inside Honen-in.

Back endpaper Quiet courtyard by the Abbot's Hall at Kennin-ji.

Page 1 A dragon emerges from a cloud at the Mirei Shigemori garden at Ryogin-an.

Pages 2–3 A garden whispers to those who listen at Komyo-in, a subtemple of Tofuku-ji.

Page 3 The entry garden of Ginkaku-ji: a stone path to perfection.

Once part of the Asian landmass, the island chain of Japan broke away from the continent and is now separated from it by the Sea of Japan. The heaving tectonic plates and volcanic activity created steeply corrugated mountains, narrow valleys, volcanoes, and shallow rivers. Even today, wisps of sulfurous steam escape from fissures beneath which smoldering magma resonates with a low rumble. With its abundance of hot springs and its fifty active volcanoes, Japan is an integral part of the Pacific Rim of Fire.

The main land masses—Hokkaido, Honshu, Shikoku, and Kyushu—along with hundreds of smaller islands strung along the archipelago, give Japan one of the world's longest coastlines.

The abundance of fertile land and variety of climates host a rich diversity of trees: pine, cedar, cypress, beech, juniper, yew, paulownia, cryptomeria, elm, magnolia, mountain cherry, camphor, mountain

Opposite above left Stone *toro* lantern and the rustic Chumon Gate beckon at Okochi Sanso.

Opposite above right Water basin with seasonal winter reflections.

Opposite below Waterfalls in the crystal-clear Nara River at Kamigamo Jinja.

Top left A path to ageless beauty at Okochi Sanso in Arashiyama.

Above Wisteria and lotus envelop Himuro Pond at Kaju-ji Temple.

Left Textured, layered, yet grounded—the world of Zen.

azalea, maple, oak, ilex, hackberry, chinquapin, andromeda, ash, and walnut. They in turn nurture a bounty of birds from continental China and beyond.

Wet-field rice cultivation began around 300 A.D. in Kyushu, spread quickly northward, and structured the land into manageable shapes for agriculture. Farmers sculpted the gentler slopes into small plots and built an elaborate canal system to irrigate the crops.

Set on the island of Honshu, in a wide basin in the middle of the archipelago, is the ancient capital of Kyoto. Sheltered on three sides by mountains, the city is wrapped in a hazy mist that promotes luxuriant floral growth and carpets the land in moss, fern, and bamboo grasses. Over mountain passes to the north lies the Sea of Japan, while the plain in the south extends to Osaka and the Inland Sea, and farther on, to the Pacific Ocean.

The high humidity also provides an ideal environment for producing silk with the flexibility needed for spinning and weaving its delicate strands. Silk is no longer produced in Kyoto, but the thousand-year-old tradition of sericulture is

Top right An agile gardener carefully shapes a *momiji* maple.

Above Autumn still life at Kamigamo Shrine.

Right Welcoming smile and brilliant azaleas at Kegon-ji Temple.

revealed in remnants of the mulberry bushes—a vital nutrient for silkworms—that have been unearthed on the plain of Kameoka, west of the city.

The Hata clan is believed to have brought silk from the Korean Peninsula when it established itself in the 4th century in the western part of what would become Kyoto. The forested basin was rich in game. Deer, bear, serow, wolves, fox, wild boar, hare, and monkeys roamed the land. The sky was dotted with cranes, ducks, egrets, and a variety of migrating birds.

By the 8th century, several capitals had been established, with one of the earliest in the fertile land around Lake Biwa. In 710, the city of Nara, just south of the lake, became the first permanent capital, with an imperial court patterned on China's. For centuries, the court adhered to the political and social dictates of Confucian cosmology, until gradually, an indigenous system evolved. A new religion, Buddhism, was also imported from China to Japan, along with carpenters to apply their superior building techniques to large temple complexes. The massive construction projects imposed a new shape on the land by

Top right Stealthy heron fishes amidst purple *shobu* irises.

Above The beginning—rocky isles emerge from the sea.

Right The principles of *yin/yang* at play—garden in Tofuku-ji.

forming wall-enclosed courtyards and elaborate structures to house sacred images. The tools and techniques were modified to build private estates for the nobles.

By 783, perhaps impelled by Nara's limited water supply, the capital was moved to Nagaoka, southwest of present-day Kyoto. After only eleven years, inauspicious events forced another relocation. Eventually, the Hata clan allowed the imperial family to hunt on its game-rich lands and to move onto its estate. The establishment in 794 of the new capital, Heian-kyo, sparked an enormous construction boom. It employed building and landscape techniques recently imported from China, while adapting them to Kyoto's environment and climate.

Like Nara, Kyoto was designed according to the geomantic dictates of *feng shui* as a grid of avenues and modeled after the older Chinese city of X'ian. The imperial court lay in the central north, at the apex of an eighty-meter-wide boulevard. The rest of the land was divided into square-shaped *cho,* within which the

Top left An artfully cultivated autumn hillside at Okochi Sanso.

Above Gardeners embark for shoreline work at Ryoan-ji's Kyoyochi Pond.

Left Tense coils of raked gravel spin perpetually.

aristocracy was allotted land to build its new estates, the dimensions of which have barely changed for a thousand years.

Now, within this context of stability, it was time for the nobles to impose their new culture on their lands. They expressed their wealth, taste, and awe of nature by creating the gardens for which Kyoto is famous today.

Initially, small hillocks and winding streams brought wild plants closer to residences, while ponds enhanced the view from a veranda or a shallow-bottomed boat. Narrow paths traversing the garden gave inhabitants varied views to stimulate their poetic tendencies and provide pleasure in a most secular manner.

Centuries later, with the introduction of Zen Buddhism, temple landscaping was designed to produce a minimum of visual stimulation, so that viewers would have an opportunity to extract and internalize meaning.

Today's landscape artists still draw from this heritage. And today's visitors, as well as future generations, are heirs to the invaluable legacy of how respect for the natural environment and the gardener's art dignify the common and make it extraordinary.

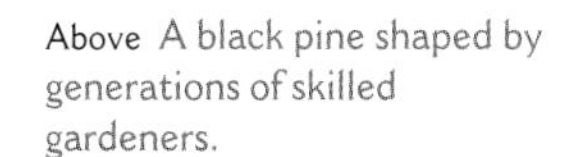

Above A black pine shaped by generations of skilled gardeners.

Left A sacred stone bounded with purifying *shimenawa* straw rope in the Shokei-en Garden at Kamigamo Jinja.

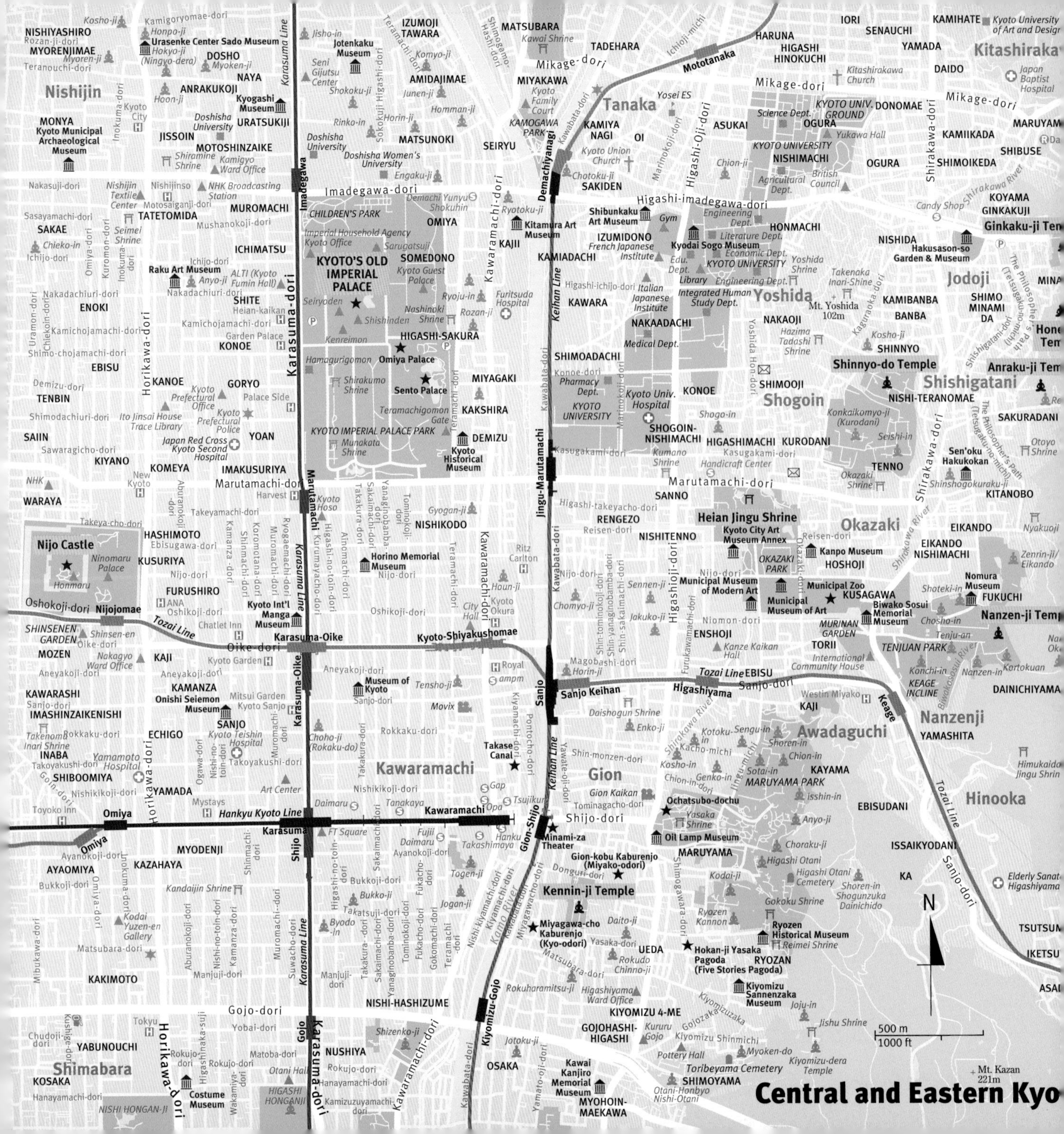

Central and Eastern Kyo
Nishijin
NISHIYASHIRO
MYORENJIMAE
Kosho-ji
Kamigoryomae-dori
Honpo-ji
Urasenke Center Sado Museum
Hokyo-ji (Ningyo-dera)
DOSHO
Myoken-ji
Myoren-ji
Teranouchi-dori
Rozan-ji-dori
NAYA
ANRAKUKOJI
Hoon-ji
Kyogashi Museum
URATSUKIJI
MONYA
Kyoto Municipal Archaeological Museum
Kyoto City
Doshisha University
JISSOIN
MOTOSHINZAIKE
Shiramine Shrine
Kamigyo Ward Office
Nakasuji-dori
Nishijin Textile Center
Nishijinso
NHK Broadcasting Station
Motosaiganji-dori
MUROMACHI
Mushanokoji-dori
Sasayamachi-dori
TATETOMIDA
SAKAE
Seimei Shrine
Chieko-in
Ichijo-dori
ICHIMATSU
Raku Art Museum
Anyo-ji
ALTI (Kyoto Fumin Hall)
Nakadachiuri-dori
SHITE
Heian-kaikan
ENOKI
Kamichojamachi-dori
Garden Palace
KONOE
Shimo-chojamachi-dori
EBISU
KANOE
GORYO
Kyoto Prefectural Office
Palace Side
TENBIN
Demizu-dori
Shimodachiuri-dori
Ito Jinsai House Trace Library
Kyoto Prefectural Police
SAIIN
YOAN
Japan Red Cross Kyoto Second Hospital
Sawaragicho-dori
KIYANO
KOMEYA
IMAKUSURIYA
NHK
New Kyoto
WARAYA
Marutamachi-dori
Harvest
Takeyamachi-dori
Takeya-cho-dori
Nijo Castle
Ninomaru Palace
Honmaru
HASHIMOTO
Ebisugawa-dori
KUSURIYA
Nijo-dori
FURUSHIRO
ANA
Oshikoji-dori
Oshokoji-dori
Nijojomae
Tozai Line
Chatlet Inn
SHINSENEN GARDEN
Shinsen-en
Oike-dori
MOZEN
Nakagyo Ward Office
KAJI
Kyoto Garden
Aneyakoji-dori
KAMANZA
Onishi Seiemon Museum
Mitsui Garden Kyoto Sanjo
KAWARASHI
Sanjo-dori
IMASHINZAIKENISHI
SANJO
Kyoto Teishin Hospital
Takenomi Inari Shrine
Rokkaku-dori
ECHIGO
INABA
Yamamoto Hospital
Takoyakushi-dori
SHIBOOMIYA
Nishikikoji-dori
YAMADA
Mystays
Toyoko Inn
Omiya
Hankyu Kyoto Line
Karasuma
Shijo
MYODENJI
AYAOMIYA
KAZAHAYA
Ayanokoji-dori
Bukkoji-dori
Kandaijin Shrine
Kodai Yuzen-en Gallery
Matsubara-dori
KAKIMOTO
Manjuji-dori
Gojo-dori
Tokyu
Chudoji-dori
YABUNOUCHI
Shimabara
KOSAKA
Hanayamachi-dori
Costume Museum
NISHI HONGAN-JI
HIGASHI HONGANJI
Horikawa-dori
Karasuma Line
Karasuma-dori
Imadegawa
Marutamachi
Karasuma-Oike
Gojo
Jisho-in
IZUMOJI TAWARA
Jotenkaku Museum
Seni Gijutsu Center
Komyo-ji
AMIDAJIMAE
Shokoku-ji
Junen-ji
Homman-ji
Rinko-in
Horin-ji
MATSUNOKI
Doshisha University
Doshisha Women's University
Engaku-ji
Imadegawa-dori
Demachi Yunyu Shokuhin
CHILDREN'S PARK
OMIYA
Imperial Household Agency Kyoto Office
Sarugatsuji
KYOTO'S OLD IMPERIAL PALACE
SOMEDONO
Kyoto Guest Palace
Seiryoden
Ryoju-in
Nashinoki Shrine
Rozan-ji
Shishinden
Kenreimon
HIGASHI-SAKURA
Hamagurigomon
Omiya Palace
Shirakumo Shrine
Sento Palace
MIYAGAKI
Teramachigomon Gate
KAKSHIRA
KYOTO IMPERIAL PALACE PARK
Munakata Shrine
DEMIZU
Kyoto Historical Museum
Kyoto Hoso
Gyogan-ji
NISHIKODO
Horino Memorial Museum
Ritz Carlton
Houn-ji
City Hall
Kyoto Okura
Kyoto Int'l Manga Museum
Kyoto-Shiyakushomae
Royal
ampm
Museum of Kyoto
Tensho-ji
Movix
Choho-ji (Rokaku-do)
Takase Canal
Kawaramachi
Art Center
Gap
Tsujikura
Daimaru
Tanakaya
Opa
FT Square
Fujii Daimaru
Hanku
Takashimaya
Togen-ji
Bukko-ji
Jogan-ji
Byodo-in
NISHI-HASHIZUME
Shizenko-ji
NUSHIYA
Otani Hall
Rokujo-dori
Kawaramachi-dori
MATSUBARA
Kawai Shrine
TADEHARA
Mikage-dori
MIYAKAWA
Kyoto Family Court
KAMOGAWA PARK
SEIRYU
Demachiyanagi
KAMIYA NAGI
Kyoto Union Church
Chotoku-ji
SAKIDEN
Ryotoku-ji
Kitamura Art Museum
KAJII
KAMIADACHI
KAWARA
Furitsuda Hospital
SHIMOADACHI
Keihan Line
Jingu-Marutamachi
Sanjo
Sanjo Keihan
Gion-Shijo
Kiyomizu-Gojo
Tanaka
Mototanaka
Ichijoji-michi
HARUNA
HIGASHI HINOKUCHI
Yosei ES
OI
ASUKAI
Chion-ji
Shibunkaku Art Museum
Gym
IZUMIDONO
French Japanese Institute
Kyodai Sogo Museum
Italian Japanese Institute
Library
Integrated Human Study Dept.
Yoshida
NAKAADACHI
Medical Dept.
Pharmacy Dept.
KYOTO UNIVERSITY
Kyoto Univ. Hospital
SHOGOIN-NISHIMACHI
KONOE
HIGASHIMACHI
KURODANI
Kumano Shrine
Handicraft Center
Marutamachi-dori
SANNO
RENGEZO
NISHITENNO
Heian Jingu Shrine
Kyoto City Art Museum Annex
OKAZAKI PARK
Kanpo Museum
Municipal Museum of Modern Art
Municipal Zoo
Municipal Museum of Art
KUSAGAWA
ENSHOJI
Kanze Kaikan Hall
TORII
Gion
Gion Kaikan
Ochatsubo-dochu
Yasaka Shrine
Oil Lamp Museum
Minami-za Theater
MARUYAMA
Gion-kobu Kaburenjo (Miyako-odori)
Kennin-ji Temple
Miyagawa-cho Kaburenjo (Kyo-odori)
Kamo River
UEDA
Hokan-ji Yasaka Pagoda (Five Stories Pagoda)
Rokudo Chinno-ji
Rokuharamitsu-ji
Higashiyama Ward Office
KIYOMIZU 4-ME
GOJOHASHI-HIGASHI
Kururu Gojo
Kiyomizu Shinmichi
Pottery Hall
OSAKA
Kawai Kanjiro Memorial Museum
SHIMOYAMA
MYOHOIN-MAEKAWA
Toribeyama Cemetery
IORI
SENAUCHI
KAMIHATE
Kyoto University of Art and Design
YAMADA
Kitashiraka
DAIDO
Kitashirakawa Church
Japan Baptist Hospital
Mikage-dori
KYOTO UNIV. GROUND
DONOMAE
Science Dept.
OGURA
Yukawa Hall
NISHIMACHI
British Council
KAMIIKADA
SHIMOIKEDA
SHIBUSE
MARUYAM
KOYAMA
GINKAKUJI
Candy Shop
Ginkaku-ji Temple
HONMACHI
NISHIDA
Hakusason-so Garden & Museum
Jodoji
KAMIBANBA
BANBA
SHIMO MINAMI DA
Mt. Yoshida 102m
NAKAOJI
SHINNYO
Shinnyo-do Temple
Anraku-ji Temple
Shishigatani
NISHI-TERANOMAE
Shogoin
SAKURADANI
TENNO
Sen'oku Hakukokan
KITANOBO
Okazaki
EIKANDO
EIKANDO NISHIMACHI
HOSHOJI
Zenrin-ji/Eikando
Nomura Museum
FUKUCHI
Biwako Sosui Memorial Museum
Nanzen-ji Temple
MURINAN GARDEN
TENJUAN PARK
International Community House
KEAGE INCLINE
DAINICHIYAMA
Keage
Nanzenji
YAMASHITA
Awadaguchi
Shoren-in
Chion-in
KAYAMA
MARUYAMA PARK
Hinooka
EBISUDANI
ISSAIKYODANI
Higashi Otani
Higashi Otani Cemetery
Elderly Sanat Higashiyama
Gokoku Shrine
Ryozen Kannon
Ryozen Historical Museum
RYOZEN
Kiyomizu Sannenzaka Museum
Kiyomizu-dera Temple
Mt. Kazan 221m
Tozai Line
Sanjo-dori
500 m
1000 ft
N

CHAPTER 1

Gardens of Central and Eastern Kyoto

At the very heart of Kyoto lies the former Imperial Palace. The emperors and courtiers who lived in the complex were subject not only to the vagaries of politics and intrigue, but to the dangers of fire and war. Each new court brought its own architectural and landscape design elements, but all were consistent with literary and artistic precepts, and most importantly, with the dictates of geomancy and ritual.

From the 6th century onward, geomancy was used to determine auspicious dates: when travelers might move or occasions should be scheduled, and even to decide the layout of a residence and, of course, its garden. The strictures included not only what physical demarcations would reshape and regulate the land, but also abstract superstitious constraints imported from China and Korea.

The divination of all these beliefs was complex and required consulting specialists, which the ritual-obsessed court did assiduously.

As the city took shape, the land was reconfigured to adhere to geomancy-determined rituals and beliefs. The system gave structure to personal lives and conferred a lasting legacy on the shape and spirit of Kyoto.

Clockwise from top left A flat-topped cone of sand at Ginkaku-ji. A young pine in the garden of Tenju-an. Ice and snow at the Silver Pavilion. *Shoji* sliding doors open on a hillside of azaleas at Anraku-ji. Silvery gravel, natural wood, and blue coordinates inside

KYOTO'S OLD IMPERIAL PALACE GARDEN

The city of Kyoto underwent an immense transition in 1868 when the imperial court was moved to Edo, which was renamed Tokyo (eastern capital). Only fifteen years earlier, Commodore Perry's black ships had opened the country to an array of Western thought and tastes that would infiltrate politics and the arts and spark deep transformations.

The old Imperial Palace and its gardens were not immune to change. The present complex was moved to Kyoto in 1788, but required considerable new construction after fire damage in 1855. Rather than an authentic reconstruction of the original buildings and gardens (better seen at Heian Shrine), the current grounds reflect an accumulation of traditional landscape concepts.

Garden views were an integral part of all but the most humble abodes, and even today, gardens provide highly desirable access to light and fresh air.

Nobles' estates, conceived on a splendid scale, conjured grand scenery: Gardens echoed distant shorelines marked by jetting rock outlines and evoked cloud-shrouded mountain scenes depicted in ancient Chinese poetry and painting. The garden was a visual reinforcement of learned aesthetic concepts beloved by the court.

The old Imperial Palace gardens remain some of the country's loveliest displays of landscape architecture. Their gardeners attract the best pupils of the art as well as the finest specimens of flora and rocks. Retaining its centuries-old design, the courtyard is a span of white, raked gravel that

Above The shadow of a curved eave intersects the courtyard's raked surface.

Opposite top Autumn as a backdrop for a magnificent gate shingled with cedar bark.

Far left A picturesque arched bridge leads to another realm.

Left A slender waterfall softens the pond's rocky edge.

Above Beyond the vermilion gate, the grounds of the old palace.

Right A graceful grey heron pauses atop a traditional stone lantern on an islet bordered by crepe myrtle in Oikeniwa Garden.

evokes the *yuniwa* (a sacred space) at shrines. Two flowering trees, a cherry and trifoliate orange, accent the quiet expanse. The area served as a site for religious ceremonies related to the court and was presided over by the emperor, once viewed as a divine descendant of the Sun Goddess. The limited grounds open to visitors are rich with moss, low sculpted pine and cedar, and other horticultural masterpieces.

Another exquisite garden within the Imperial Park is at Sento Gosho, the villa of retired Emperor Gomizuno (1596–1680). Constructed in 1600, the

Above Struts prop a precious, aged maple.

Right A moss-rimmed bridge with a simple wooden railing introduces a touch of rusticity, an essential element, even in imperial gardens.

Left The sleek new Geihinkan is Kyoto's State Guest House for visiting dignitaries, built in 2005 inside the spacious grounds of Kyoto Gyoen National Garden.

Below A *wasen* pleasure boat for VIP excursions on the Geihinkan's pond.

Bottom A blossoming cherry tree overhangs the precisely laid *suhama* stone shore of South Pond at Sento Gosho.

original buildings were destroyed several times by fire, but the stroll garden remains. It is an aesthetic miracle of quietude, simplicity, and beauty in the middle of the city.

After receiving permission from the Imperial Household Agency, visitors can take an hour-long tour, which leads across a trellis-covered bridge that is magnificent in May when it is lush with tendrils of purple and white wisteria. Recalling thousand-year-old Heian gardens, the paths wind past a slightly elevated waterfall that empties into a large pond, once used for boating. The grounds feature azalea, boxwood bushes, and hedges of wild mountain rose and camellia distributed and sculpted with Zen-like restraint.

Next to a shoreline is a resting place of perfectly rounded stones, a gift from the lord of a clan in eastern Japan. Each stone was valued for its shape and color, wrapped individually in silk and presented to the apprecia-tive emperor.

Guests are encouraged not to dawdle along the paths. But it is nearly impossible not to linger, as the designers intended, and to marvel at the ingenuity of the plan and the exquisite scenic perspective from each view—a privilege previously granted only to members of the imperial court.

NIJO CASTLE GARDEN

When the warlord Tokugawa Ieyasu took control of Japan, he moved the capital to Edo, now named Tokyo.

But in 1603, for administrative purposes and to retain his powerful connections to the court, Tokugawa built Nijo Castle in Kyoto. Not designed for military purposes, its buildings resemble no other fortress

Opposite above The castle's gleaming southeast turret, a beloved Kyoto landmark.

Opposite below The remains of a turret overlook the castle granary in early spring.

Left A mother and grandmother take a toddler on her first cherry-blossom viewing.

Below Sculptural evidence of Japanese gardeners' artistic talents in Ninomaru Garden, bordering Ninomaru-goten Palace, a National Treasure.

Above A single pine tree requires a whole day's attention by a gardener.

in Japan, where frequent warfare dictated architecture and necessitated construction on strategic, elevated sites.

The Tokugawas were warriors, but they wanted Nijo to be a monument to their refinement as well as their power. The moat and donjons, then, are mainly symbolic displays of military strength; the gardens make a show of economic and martial power. As intended, the grounds and buildings successfully combine the aesthetics and culture of the court with manifestations of power. Famed artists of the Kano School captured this fusion in the castle's screens and doors, painted with lavish portraits of fierce animals such as eagles and tigers.

The gardens, too, have a military feel, but are framed, as

in ancient courtly tradition, by the doorways of the corridors that circle the main building. Large stones and low trees—including exotic cycads brought from more tropical climes—give this garden a masculine feel and also help prevent intruders from approaching unseen.

The back garden to the west has several large ponds, which are set among low, grass-covered mounds interspersed with resplendent pines and gatherings of boulders at water's edge.

The garden to the north has more recent plantings, including large Japanese pagoda trees *(enju)* rarely seen in gardens. Their dominant shape and height, not easily incorporated into smaller gardens, embody the comfortable spaciousness of wealth and power.

While expressing the confidence and strength of military rulers, Nijo's overall effect is softened in spring by bountiful plantings of cherry trees. Lighted displays of the trees in bloom are one of April's biggest nighttime attractions. The soft loveliness, set against the muscular architecture, highlights the disparate yet harmonized sides of Kyoto's former warlords and the castle they built.

Above left A wild duck navigates the placid inner moat below the Honmaru's steeply sloped stone defensive wall.

Above right A grey heron patrols its watery domain.

Left Pavilion with a view, a pink cascade concealing Honmaru West Bridge.

Right Vertical rocks form the pond's bank.

Middle right *Shimoyoke* 'frost protectors' of braided straw for subtropical cycad sago palms.

Above A stone water basin in the Seiryu-en tea garden denotes a nearby teahouse.

HEIAN JINGU SHRINE GARDEN

Entering this shrine's garden is like floating into a lush floral bed. In April when hanging cherry trees shelter the visitor under graceful blossom-filled limbs, Heian Jingu might be the most inviting place on earth. For a few moments, the world becomes a diaphanous realm of pinks.

The relatively new shrine and garden, modeled on the original palace, were constructed in 1892 to commemorate the eleven hundredth anniversary of the founding of Kyoto, "The Capital of Tranquility and Peace." Reconstructed on a two-thirds scale, shrine and grounds retained the symmetrical style of Chinese courtyards with a main hall flanked by two smaller, attached halls painted brilliant vermilion and crowned with green roof tiles.

The vast front expanse of white gravel represents an ancient, sacred area *(yuniwa)* where visitors may approach the gods. Two trees, a cherry and a trifoliate orange, are symbolic floral representations of the geomantic principles of *in* and *yo,* dark and light, female and male.

A gate to the left of the main buildings opens onto the renowned stroll garden. Court life twelve hundred years ago emphasized learning Chinese language, literature, and poetry, as well as performing rituals, many of which were conducted in the garden. Geomancy guided the hand of the nobles who took great pride in constructing their gardens to welcome auspicious spirits and rebuff inauspicious ones. Ponds were

Far left Byakkoro Tower's turrets emerge above a diaphanous pink universe.

Left A sprig of cherry at the pond's edge.

Opposite below Too tempting not to touch.

Above Dragon-tail stepping stone pillars of Garyukyo Bridge in Soryu Pond.

Left Echoes of greenery in the pond.

Below Oten-mon, the Divine Gate leads to a vast gravel courtyard and the Great Audience Hall, Daigokuden.

an essential feature, as were slender streams. Their curving passage irrigated the grounds while evoking scenes of distant places and feeding the poetic muse of the inhabitants.

Leaving the flat, white courtyard, the visitor descends gentle stairs to a path that passes under the billowing cherry blossoms of spring or the russet and peach-colored leaves of autumn. Soft mounds of moss

mingle along the path with delicate plantings of flora. Many of these plants have medicinal or culinary uses and are represented in ancient paintings and poetry. The grey stone bridges over a stream provide a cool counterpoint to the lush landscape.

After the path winds under wisteria trellises, the view widens to reveal a landscape of large ponds fringed with thousands of irises. Throughout late May and June, they bloom resplendently in shades from soft lavender to deep violet, interspaced with pure white. One ancient variety is carefully removed and replanted each year to preserve the purity of the species. Throughout July and August, the palette changes to the bright hues of the water lilies that cover the pond. The round steppingstones that once served as the pillars of an old bridge curve, sensuous as a dragon's tail, through the water.

To the north, the hydrangeas that bloom in late spring fill the off-path areas with blues and pinks.

A turn east reveals a Chinese-style bridge, once part of a former palace, that spans the water, allowing visitors to linger for a last look at the pond. Its smooth surface is disturbed only by the occasional emergence of resident koi and turtles, and by the graceful reflection of the carved phoenix atop the covered bridge.

Above, clockwise from top left Radiant maple leaves. Sensuous surface of a banana leaf. Vermilion pavilion with green roof tiles and a cherry-blossom topping. Foliage, once above, now floats below.

Ogawa Jihei (1860–1933), a prolific landscape artist who planned many of the estates in this area of town, is credited with the design. The garden, although it has been replanted and altered to suit modern tastes and horticultural advances, is one of the most beautiful examples of an ancient stroll garden. It immerses visitors in a holistic experience that melds poetry and landscape.

Opposite bottom Pampered pines with wooden supports to brace an impressive network of long contorted branches.

Above Architectural elegance—the pond's covered bridge.

Right A chance to reflect from a favorite rest spot.

KENNIN-JI TEMPLE GARDEN

On the south border of Gion, Kennin-ji sits at the heart of Kyoto. The city has many classic Zen gardens, but Kennin-ji's rock and sand landscape—free from the distractions that fragrant or colorful flowers might bring—offers a respite from the noisy, bustling world just outside its grounds and an opportunity for quiet contemplation.

This Rinzai Zen sect temple recently redesigned its gardens using splendid examples of the enduring tradition of *karesansui* (dry gardens). Rather than delight the senses, *karesansui* settles the heart and clears the mind by directing thoughts inward.

Designers of Zen gardens were greatly influenced by 14th and 15th century Chinese Sung Dynasty ink brush painting. In these misty and elegant works, clouds drift among distant, craggy mountains that dwarf

Opposite above Unpapered lattice doors frame a view of the main garden.

Opposite below Listening to the silence.

Left An appreciative kimono-clad bevy of young women.

Below Meticulous care transforms moss into more than a simple groundcover.

Above A skillfully wielded rake creates undulating impressions.

the cliff-hugging hermitages of the immortals, reducing the sentient world to insignificance. Strong strokes of black ink dissolve into wispy grey as the brush leaks its life-giving moisture onto the rice paper. The viewer's small place within this universe provided a template for Zen gardeners.

The temple's *karesansui* garden is sparsely landscaped with swirls of raked gravel surrounding a low rock dotted with a miniscule patch of moss. Another garden in the complex features a moss-covered rise set with several upright stones representing Shakyamuni Buddha and two attendants. Slender maple boughs paint the moss with filtered light.

Yet another garden contains a perfect circle of raked gravel.

With no footprint or hint of human intervention, it leads the viewer to ponder how it was made and what it might signify. Like all Zen gardens, Kennin-ji's are designed to aid meditation by challenging viewers to look within and glean knowledge from the resonance of what lies before them.

The gardens of Kennin-ji have a pleasingly modern flavor. Even though confined by walls, they seem more expansive than older, more traditional gardens. But they still appear unbridled by the mundane—just as Zen gardens ought to be.

Top Elegant guests, elegant garden.

Above, from left to right Waves, chevrons, circles—all part of the Zen gardener's template.

Right The soothing sound of water flowing into the basin.

Opposite above left A single rock—a gardener's gift to the tree?

Opposite above right Horizontal lines, wave-patterned tiles, and a profusion of cherry blossoms.

Opposite below A moment too beautiful to pass unrecorded.

NANZEN-JI TEMPLE GARDEN

Resting in the shade of the Eastern Mountains, Nanzen-ji provides a pleasing contrast to the austere gardens typical of Rinzai-sect Zen temples. Four of the twelve subtemples are open to the public, as are some lovely stroll gardens.

Once the villa of Emperor Kameyama (1249–1305), the grounds were converted into a temple after his abdication in 1274. The garden around the main quarters of the *hojo* (abbot's quarters) retains the spaciousness appropriate to an imperial residence.

Sadly, most of the original temples were destroyed during the tumultuous wars of the 15th century. Their renewal in 1611 by the Tokugawa warlord occurred when *karesansui* (dry rock and sand gardens) were reshaping the land within Zen temples. An expanse of raked gravel or sand around a cluster of rocks or clipped shrubbery reflected the Zen emphasis on austerity, emptiness, and self-control. The intentionally calming, even somber, mood allows visitors to sit in appreciation and provides an opportunity to tame a restless mind.

The subtemple Nanzen-in has been revived with both a contemplative garden on its eastern side and a stroll garden on the south. On the east, a neat sequence of diamond-shaped stones set in a trail of moss is as strikingly simple as it is pleasing. The soft, earthen path through the south garden crosses a pond and leads to an Edo period-style stroll garden. Older trees form a canopy that filters mottled light onto a groundcover of moss.

Even in a city filled with famous gardens, the subtemple of Konchi-in is renowned. Kobori Enshu (1579–1647), a brilliant arbiter of taste and garden design, is credited with planning and designing this gem, as well as many of Kyoto's most famous gardens.

When the early Zen gardens were taking shape, it was common for the head abbot to collaborate with painters and

Opposite above Shingled with cedar bark, Tenju-an's roof rises above the wooded Eastern Mountains.

Opposite below The new side garden flanks the approach to Nanzen-in.

Above The open gravel-raked courtyard of the abbot's quarters.

Below A neighborhood resident savors her morning meditation on an arched stone bridge spanning a pond of fragrant pink lotus.

gardeners. Enshu and the head priest, who was appointed by the Tokugawa government, were members of the same class and worked together to create a dynamic landscape statement.

Over the centuries, as the style became codified, some professional gardeners and caretakers initiated replantings and made changes to Enshu's art that diminished his original verve. Konchi-in, though, remains one of several gardens that still reveal the master's hand. The massive stonework and well-sculpted trees that balance the stretch of raked sand in the foreground are characteristic of Enshu's work.

The garden also features the conceit of *tsuru-kame* (paired crane and tortoise), an Asian symbol of longevity and immortality—concepts valued by the warrior class.

Above Translucent spring light illuminates the approach to the Sanmon Gate.

Below, from left to right Textured bark of a red pine. Slow approach to a Zen garden. Crimson veil of maple leaves.

Above Waiting for a breeze.

Left Snowfall highlights the distinctive coloration of a statuesque *akamatsu* red pine at Konchi-in.

Below Isles of moss flank the covered walkway in the abbot's quarters.

SHINNYO-DO HERMITAGE GARDEN

Buddhism, which reached Japan in the 6th century, was such a strong influence on Nara period Emperor Shotoku Taishi that he made this foreign belief system the state religion. The increasingly widespread acceptance of different sects, a new lexicon of saints, and the study of sutras contributed to a new culture that changed the social practices of the court and eventually of society as a whole.

Tendai was one of the earliest sects to wield sway over the newly founded capital of Kyoto. Soon, the thousand temples of Enryaku-ji, the sect's headquarters, spread across the velvet, green folds of Mt. Hiei. In 984, one of Enryaku-ji's priests left and moved to Mt. Yoshida,

a hillside outside the eastern border of the capital. There he built a small hermitage, which became Shinnyo-do. This temple had land covering much of the hillside and featured several notable gardens.

The death of Shakyamuni is memorialized at several Kyoto temples that display large scrolls depicting his death twenty-four hundred years ago. The historical Buddha is pictured as a reclining figure surrounded by his disciples; his mother, bearing an urn containing an elixir; and twelve creatures gathered to honor him.

Shinnyo-do's massive, hanging scroll of this scene, *nehanzu*, is mounted within the temple, and in 1990, a garden was constructed to complement it.

The gardens are an example of how Buddhism conveyed its tenets not only through formal

Opposite left A new garden by Chisao Shigemori, grandson of Mirei Shigemori, incorporates the Mitsui family crest.

Opposite right Young eyes learn to appreciate.

Above Early morning view of the garden of the reclining Buddha.

Right The three-tiered Shinnyo-do pagoda.

art and religious study, but also though its gardens. Honoring this concept, gardeners have constructed elevated mounds to resemble the mountainous terrain of Chinese cosmology and chosen rocks to represent Buddhist figures.

Shinnyo-do is a fine example of how Buddhist teaching reshapes a plot of land. Groupings of rocks that represent Buddha's disciples and mother stand near a long, low mound of moss that outlines the reclining Buddha. Beyond, in the distance, historic Mt. Daimonji is incorporated into the scene, enhancing the already stirring effect.

Memorials to Buddha's death are held in mid-to-late March, and on August 16, when the figure *dai* is set alight with fire to guide ancestral souls back to the nether world.

Throughout the year, the garden is a tranquil complement to the *nehanzu* scroll within the temple.

Left The Hondo's great wooden veranda overlooks vivid *momiji* maple trees in the surrounding courtyard.

Below left Svelte maples line the approach to the sutra hall.

Below right Stones, softened by moss, represent the reclining Buddha, with attendant disciples and animals paying their respects.

Right Each visit to the Nirvana Garden is unique.

Above An elevated corridor connects the Shoin Study and the Hondo Hall, offering a sheltered experience during any weather, any season.

Below Rain spouts in a stylized rain-cloud motif hang from the roof's eave.

ANRAKU-JI TEMPLE GARDEN

Many of the temples nestled in the foothills of Kyoto's Eastern Mountains have a spiritual relationship with Enryaku-ji, a Tendai temple atop Mt. Hiei. Tendai was one of the first sects to take root in Kyoto. Although many monks adhered to its spiritual path, others, notably Honen (1133–1212), questioned the sect's tenets.

Tendai Buddhists believe that enlightenment requires vigorous effort and meditation. Honen, however, taught that rebirth in the Pure Land relied on the compassionate Amida Buddha, and salvation was attained by chanting "*Namu Amida Butsu.*"

This simple belief appealed greatly to the general population, which had been excluded from spiritual attainment by the lack of education needed to read obscure texts and chant complex sutras. Honen made religion accessible, and his sect, Jodo-shu, spread.

Honen's pupils, Anraku and Juren, converted two of the emperor's court ladies, but the unknown manner of their recruitment raised suspicions. In 1207 the monks were condemned to death and beheaded.

Their graves lie in this humble, little temple, set far from downtown, in a spot that is rustic even along Kyoto's pastoral Philosopher's Walk.

The winding road that passes Honen-in and Anraku-ji is just wide enough for the occasional car, which pushes pedestrians to hug the road's edge. Set in a quiet area, Anraku-ji is open to the public only twice a year—in spring when its azaleas and camellias bloom, and in autumn when its foliage glows with color.

For half the year, the shadow of the Eastern Mountains shades

Above Stone path to the main hall.

Opposite above A long flight of shallow steps: the approach to the thatched-roof entrance gate.

Opposite below Careful trimming highlights the low lantern.

Above An ancient maple illuminates the temple entrance.

Below Famed for its dense growth of azalea bushes, the temple opens to visitors in spring and autumn.

Above A temple monk attends to his duties.
Right The view beyond the covered inner corridor.
Below The hushed light of early morning in the maple-bordered grounds.

the temple grounds until late morning, ensuring a thick carpet of moss. A double *mokkoku* tree (Japanese cleyera) of considerable age stands in front of the main hall, its root network pillowed in star moss. Several moss-lined, dry "streambeds" on the grounds feature rocks attractively mottled with a patina of age.

The artfully sculpted azalea and camellia bushes testify to the gardener's skill, and the color of their blooms to nature's generosity.

The peaceful beauty of this setting remains a poignant reminder of the lives of those who lie here.

Left Stone image of Jizo stands before a double-trunked Japanese cleyera tree.

Right, clockwise from top left Gnarled tree roots. Wave-patterned tile in an earthen wall. Fallen leaves rest on a bamboo grass groundcover. A linear bamboo fence.

Below Coming soon: a rich fusion of pink, peach, fuchsia, and deep coral.

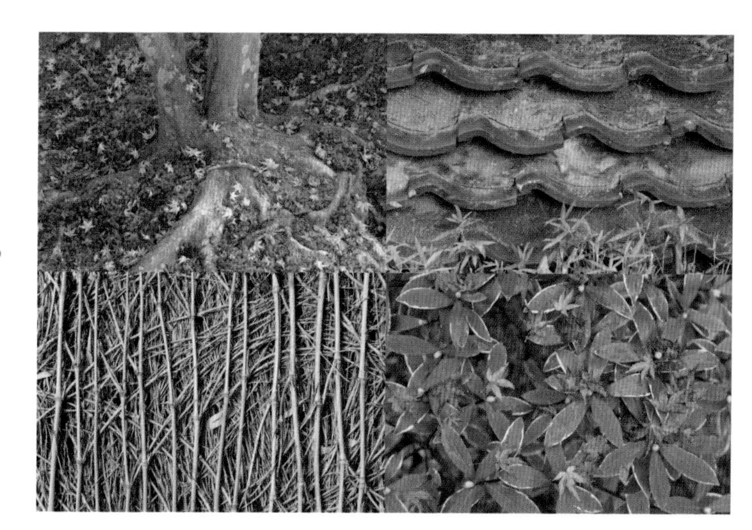

HONEN-IN TEMPLE GARDEN

Below left Although it lies within the city, the atmosphere is rustic.
Below right An artfully placed leaf directs the quiet flow of water.

The towering bamboo and pine trees that shade the stone walkway to this humble Jodo sect temple have a soothing effect on visitors, who approach with hushed voices. Beside these trees, arching boughs of bush camellia form a canopy and in March and early April carpet the ground with scarlet blossoms.

The priest Honen (1133–1212) established the Jodo sect of Buddhism during a period of upheaval marked by famine, epidemics, and natural disasters. Until then, religion had been the provenance of the nobles, not commoners. Honen, moved by the widespread suffering in this unstable era, aimed to provide a religious path—as simple as chanting the invocation "*Namu Amida Butsu*"—for everyone to attain salvation. Initially, Jodo-shu was persecuted by more prominent sects. Eventually, with the intervention of the Tokugawa shogunate, it grew to become one of the largest sects in Japan.

The 13th century also saw rising military power, accompanied by the Zen Buddhist tenets of austerity, simplicity, and self-discipline—which arose partly in reaction to the opulence of the imperial court.

Honen-in provides a good example of the era's ascendant

Zen aesthetic. The garden contains a mixture of design elements, from the long and verdant entrance, to the elegantly simple thatched-roof gate, to the stark mounds of raised and raked sand immediately within. The designs may reflect the seasons or a spiritual conundrum *(koan)* that a teacher gives an acolyte. They might depict waves, clouds, flower patterns. Or the universe itself. It is in the eye of the beholder to decide.

Farther on, a low, stone bridge spans paths and a koi-filled pond. The Eastern Mountains limit the edge of the garden,

Opposite above Visitors at the thatched-roof gate.

Top Sculpted mounds of sand—a plane for the Zen mind.

Above Masses of April-blooming camellia trees form a canopy over the entrance walk—two blossoms adorn this water basin.

Left Moss grows profusely in the foothills of the Eastern Mountains.

while the deep shadows they cast over the grounds nurture a fine covering of moss.

When some of the present buildings were added in the 17th century, the new formations introduced into the gardens retained the sense of solitude and tranquility of the original grounds.

Left A cherry blossom drifts on sculpted sand.

Below left Heavy, hinged wooden doors swung open for visitors.

Below right Fallen leaves drift onto maple-leaf patterned sand.

Left The inner garden boasts an unusual multi-colored camellia tree.

Right above Lichens lighten the slender tree trunks.

Right below Erosion exposes a fine network of tree roots.

Below A touch of wilderness permeates the grounds and its leaf-covered pond.

GINKAKU-JI PURE LAND GARDEN

An earthly paradise was the model for this temple's garden, as for its predecessors, Kinkaku-ji and Byodo-in. Reaching back through the centuries, Buddhist teachings revealed that Amida Buddha, the compassionate Buddha, would descend to help those who invoked his name and welcome them to the Pure Land.

Built at the foot rather than atop a mountain, the temple

was meant to be accessible to all who believed in the benevolent nature of this deity.

Ashikaga Yoshimasa built this estate in 1482 as a retreat from the demands of ruling a city plagued by warfare, poverty, and anguish. During his residence, the garden was constructed, and on his death, it was converted into the Zen temple Jisho-ji.

For today's visitor the very first hint of the richness of this emperor's former estate is the elaborate hedge that manifests the concept of *shin-gyo-so,* the three levels of formality. The bottom, the most informal layer, is constructed of irregular stone; the middle is a vertical bamboo fence; and the top is a several-meter-high hedge, kept in meticulous shape even after hundreds of years. A graceful cusped window frames the visitor's next view: an intriguing juxtaposition of raked sand, devoid of any growth, set against a voluptuous backdrop of woodland.

The pond serves several purposes. On a practical level, it gives the garden the illusion of greater depth and space by reflecting the bordering greenery. It also symbolizes the expanse between this world and the Pure Land. But beyond aesthetics and conveying the

Left Shaded hillside paths offer views of elegant rooflines.

Below The densely packed sand cone takes years of practice to sculpt—a test of a monk's patience and steady hand.

Bottom Stone, bamboo, and hedge indicate three elements of formality that are an integral part of Japanese aesthetics.

Opposite above Although the garden layout is complex, the eye is instantly drawn to the truncated cone of compact sand relegating the Silver Pavilion to the background.

Opposite below The graceful lines of the cusped window contrast with long, straight rows of two-toned, raked sand.

spiritual notions of transience, the pond provided more sensual pleasures. It gave residents the opportunity to drift in a shallow-bottomed boat to view the landscape from a water-born perspective. That gentle scene, along with the garden's almost pure white sand on full-moon nights inspired some to indulge their romantic tendencies.

Since Ginkaku-ji attained World Heritage Site status, it has tried to accommodate the increased number of visitors by expanding the walks along the foothills. This emphasis has made it more of a strolling garden than a contemplative one. Paths lead to the Moon Washing Waterfall and farther up, reveal views of the delicately constructed pavilion below. The temple's silvery glow in moon-light, while not actually from a covering of that precious metal, nonetheless dazzles beholders.

Left, from top to bottom The intended meaning of the flattened cone top remains a mystery to this day. A patina-embellished stone within the raked sand. The pleasing geometric design clears the mind.

Above Winter sunlight illuminates the Kuri Hall's architectural symmetry, accentuated by twisted pines in the outer garden.

Left A grey heron takes flight.

Top left The symmetrical lines of the sculpted mound and the forested hills beyond create a desired tension.

Above A raked plane of sand stands out in juxtaposition to the wooded mountainside.

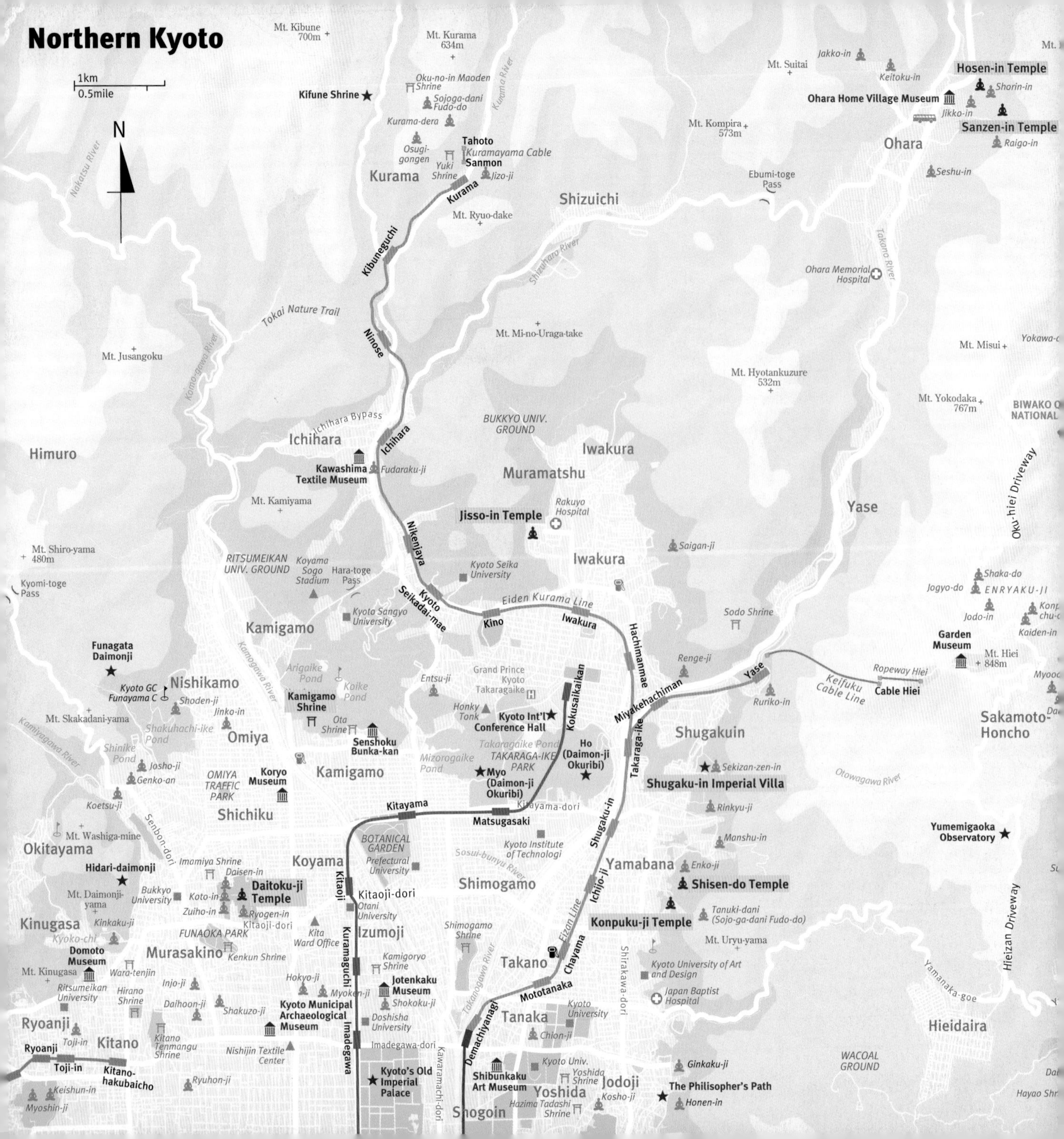

Northern Kyoto
1km
0.5mile
N
Mt. Kibune 700m
Mt. Kurama 634m
Kifune Shrine
Oku-no-in Maoden Shrine
Sojoga-dani Fudo-do
Kurama-dera
Osugi-gongen
Tahoto
Kuramayama Cable
Sanmon
Yuki Shrine
Jizo-ji
Kurama
Kurama River
Nakatsu River
Mt. Ryuo-dake
Shizuichi
Mt. Suitai
Jakko-in
Keitoku-in
Hosen-in Temple
Shorin-in
Ohara Home Village Museum
Jikko-in
Sanzen-in Temple
Raigo-in
Ohara
Seshu-in
Mt. Kompira 573m
Ebumi-toge Pass
Shizuhara River
Takano River
Ohara Memorial Hospital
Kibuneguchi
Tokai Nature Trail
Ninose
Mt. Mi-no-Uraga-take
Mt. Jusangoku
Kamo-gawa River
Mt. Misui
Yokawa-
Mt. Hyotankuzure 532m
Mt. Yokodaka 767m
BIWAKO
NATIONAL
Ichihara Bypass
Ichihara
BUKKYO UNIV. GROUND
Himuro
Iwakura
Kawashima Textile Museum
Fudaraku-ji
Muramatshu
Oku-hiei Driveway
Mt. Kamiyama
Jisso-in Temple
Rakuyo Hospital
Yase
Nikenjaya
Mt. Shiro-yama 480m
RITSUMEIKAN UNIV. GROUND
Koyama Sogo Stadium
Hara-toge Pass
Kyoto Seika University
Iwakura
Saigan-ji
Kyomi-toge Pass
Shaka-do
Jogyo-do
ENRYAKU-JI
Kyoto Seikadai-mae
Eiden Kurama Line
Kyoto Sangyo University
Kino
Iwakura
Sodo Shrine
Jodo-in
Kaiden-in
Kamigamo
Hachimanmae
Garden Museum
Mt. Hiei 848m
Funagata Daimonji
Kamogawa River
Arigaike Pond
Koike Pond
Entsu-ji
Grand Prince Kyoto Takaragaike
Renge-ji
Yase
Ropeway Hiei
Keifuku Cable Line
Cable Hiei
Kyoto GC Funayama C
Nishikamo
Shoden-ji
Kamigamo Shrine
Kokusaikaikan
Miyakehachiman
Ruriko-in
Mt. Skakadani-yama
Jinko-in
Honky Tonk
Kyoto Int'l Conference Hall
Omiya
Ota Shrine
Senshoku Bunka-kan
Takaragaike Pond
TAKARAGA-IKE PARK
Ho (Daimon-ji Okuribi)
Takaraga-ike
Shugakuin
Sakamoto-Honcho
Kamiyagawa River
Shakuhachi-ike Pond
Shinike Pond
Josho-ji
Genko-an
OMIYA TRAFFIC PARK
Koryo Museum
Kamigamo
Mizorogaike Pond
Myo (Daimon-ji Okuribi)
Sekizan-zen-in
Shugaku-in Imperial Villa
Otowagawa River
Koetsu-ji
Senbon-dori
Shichiku
Kitayama
Matsugasaki
Kitayama-dori
Shugaku-in
Rinkyu-ji
Mt. Washiga-mine
Okitayama
BOTANICAL GARDEN
Kyoto Institute of Technologi
Manshu-in
Yumemigaoka Observatory
Hidari-daimonji
Imamiya Shrine
Daisen-in
Koyama
Prefectural University
Sosui-bunyu River
Yamabana
Enko-ji
Mt. Daimonji-yama
Bukkyo University
Koto-in
Daitoku-ji Temple
Kitaoji
Kitaoji-dori
Shimogamo
Ichijo-ji
Shisen-do Temple
Zuiho-in
Ryogen-in
Otani University
Tanuki-dani (Sojo-ga-dani Fudo-do)
Kinugasa
Kinkaku-ji
Kitaoji-dori
Kita Ward Office
Konpuku-ji Temple
Kyoko-chi
FUNAOKA PARK
Izumoji
Shimogamo Shrine
Eizan Line
Mt. Uryu-yama
Hieizan Driveway
Domoto Museum
Murasakino
Kenkun Shrine
Kuramaguchi
Takano
Chayama
Shirakawa-dori
Kyoto University of Art and Design
Yamanaka-goe
Mt. Kinugasa
Wara-tenjin
Kamigoryo Shrine
Takanogawa River
Ritsumeikan University
Hirano Shrine
Injo-ji
Hokyo-ji
Myoken-ji
Jotenkaku Museum
Mototanaka
Japan Baptist Hospital
Daihoon-ji
Shakuzo-ji
Kyoto Municipal Archaeological Museum
Shokoku-ji
Ryoanji
Toji-in
Kitano
Kitano Tenmangu Shrine
Doshisha University
Imadegawa
Demachiyanagi
Tanaka
Kyoto University
Hieidaira
Chion-ji
Imadegawa-dori
Nishijin Textile Center
Kawaramachi-dori
WACOAL GROUND
Ryoanji
Toji-in
Kitano-hakubaicho
Keishun-in
Ryuhon-ji
Kyoto's Old Imperial Palace
Shibunkaku Art Museum
Kyoto Univ.
Yoshida Shrine
Jodoji
Ginkaku-ji
The Philisopher's Path
Myoshin-ji
Yoshida
Kosho-ji
Honen-in
Hazima Tadashi Shrine
Shogoin
Hayao Shr

CHAPTER 2

Gardens of Northern Kyoto

The thirty-six peaks along the Eastern Mountains run from Kyoto's southern limits north to Mt. Hiei. Thickly forested slopes bestow fine, seasonal displays and have long inspired art for standing screens, painted sliding doors, and kimono design.

The abundance of streams along the hilly terrain ensures luxuriant humidity for the gardens that lie downstream. The shadow cast by Mt. Hiei, the highest peak in this range, nurtures abundant greenery for wildlife, including deer, wild boar, serow, and monkeys. Because the region's temples and estates lie outside the city's original grid, they were free to expand generously, without the spatial constraints imposed on inner-city residences.

Clockwise from top left Local residents seek relief from the summer heat in the outer garden at Kamigamo Shrine. Symbol of Japanese gods' descent to the country on its mountaintops. A Zen monk performs daily gardening chores at Myoshin-ji. Jisso-in's contemporary front garden. The thatched Robaikan Gate and snow-covered entry garden at Shisen-do.

KONPUKU-JI POET'S GARDEN

The entrance is unobtrusive, even retiring, but the small hillside garden bears an impressive artistic legacy. During his sojourn around Japan, Basho (1644–1724) stayed on the grounds in the thatched-roof cottage now named Basho-an, after the poet. Later, the painter and poet Buson (1716–1784), dismayed by the condition of the buildings at the time of his visit, restored many of them. His grave and those of his disciples are on the hillside.

Japanese poetry and gardening have a millennia-old relationship. In the Heian period, aristocrats expressed their poetic nature by building gardens that used literary images to stir emotions. And by settling the mind and soothing the spirit, the garden was a perfect venue for composing a

Right Interplay of patterns: calico cat and stone path.

Below An unvarnished plank and bamboo veranda with a sprinkle of maple leaves.

Opposite above Stone placement in paths represents different levels of formality.

Opposite below A water basin shaped like an ancient coin.

Above A visit to Basho's hut on a crisp, autumn day.

Right Densely planted with three kinds of azalea, the approaches to Basho's hut and Buson's grave are hilly and narrow.

short verse. At poetry gatherings, guests fell under the spell of the beauty and inscribed verse sentiments to mark the occasion.

Basho, who espoused a simple life, still captures Japan's imagination and respect. Spare and clean, his haiku descriptions of his travels reveal extravagant depth and beauty. Like Basho himself, the plant named after him—a lean, banana-like tree—exhibits modest grace. This aesthetic extends to Konpuku-ji's gardens.

The few flowering plants, azaleas, climb the slope behind the main hall in rounded rows.

Left The moist sheen of a stone path—simple yet superbly elegant.

Below A modest thatched hut for literary giants.

Bottom A snowy blanket for Basho-an, where the legendary haiku poet encamped in 1670.

Two of the azalea varieties that bloom on the hilly garden from March to April—*tsutsuji* and *mitsuba tsutsuji*—are gorgeous and showy. The third, *dodan tsutsuji,* bears only discrete clusters of tiny, white flowers. It is only in fall, then, that this modest plant reveals its true beauty in the vivid hues of its leaves.

A hillside path leads to Buson's grave and Basho's charming, thatched cottage. The serene and simple grounds nurture a quietude that feeds the poetic soul.

Above A thicket fence and a bamboo well cover show elements essential to the gardener's trade.

Right, from top to bottom A drop of color on raked gravel furrows in the *karesansui* dry landscape garden. Camellia blossoms brighten an expanse of moss. Bundles of mixed branches form a fence-as-garden ornament. The symbiotic relation of stone and veranda support. Maple leaves entangled in *higegusa* grass.

SHISEN-DO VILLA GARDEN

A long slope rises from Kyoto's eastern-most street to this mountain temple, where the air is cooler and fresher. The ascent is lined with residents' potted plants and country-style front gardens. The Eastern Mountains continue to shade the byways well after noon, until the setting sun illuminates this area in a warm glow.

Shisen-do was the estate of Ishikawa Jozan (1583–1672), a literati who—after the Tokugawa shogunate exiled him—lived here for forty years, practicing the arts of tea, poetry, and garden design.

His life's work is evident in his residence and its magnificent garden. In May, when an array of round, sculpted azalea bushes blooms beside an expanse of flat white sand, the visitor is treated to a vivid and compelling scene.

Walking the entrance path is like traveling through a darkened tunnel and emerging into brilliant light. The narrow, winding approach is shrouded by immense, deciduous trees that block the sun, encouraging visitors to walk carefully, with eyes cast down.

Then the garden opens up to display a rich palette of color

Opposite left In traditional indigo farmers' garb, a woman heads to work.

Opposite right Splendid in shape and color—a spring azalea.

Above Horticultural artistry, the product of centuries of pruning and sculpting.

Right Subtle shades of stone form the path to the temple entrance.

and form. Although more expansive than the traditionally intimate tea garden, it nonetheless recalls this genre's formal design. A tall, rounded water basin stands by the veranda so guests may rinse their hands and mouth—an act of purification connected with the tea ceremony's spiritual nature.

Most tea gardens, in accordance with Zen thought, cultivate simplicity rather than stimulation. They favor quiet plantings such as bamboo, pine, and camellia—although they do allow the occasional flash of color in *satsuki* and *tsutsuji*, two azalea varieties. In spring, then, Shisen-do's azalea display seems opulent, but the garden resumes its more austere face during other seasons. In winter, a large, white camellia dominates and delights the connoisseur's eye with its simple blooms.

To please the ear, a delicate tube of bamboo fills with flowing water and then taps sharply against a stone as it tips over, emptying its contents into a stream. This device began as more than an ornament. Its sound also discourages deer and wild boar from entering the garden. The woods that harbor these wild creatures surround and shade the clipped shrubbery. In spring the forest complements the formal garden with vivid green; in fall its backdrop adds a glow of scarlet maples.

Above A sudden summer downpour breaks the stillness and enriches the greenery.

Far right, from top to bottom Bamboo gutters soften the sound of rain. A young bamboo grove frames the latticed paper window. Steppingstones, each selected for shape and color.

Left Snow enhances the villa's innate quietude.

Right Sublime touch of autumn.

Below Shisen-do's dark interior provides an intentionally startling contrast to the bright expanse of white sand.

SHUGAKU-IN IMPERIAL VILLA GARDEN

A border of terraced, imperial rice fields and a backdrop of the Eastern Mountains gives this imperial villa its distinctly rustic setting. The grounds are vast yet airy, with stretches of filtered sunlight highlighting the mossy groundcover. On the lower level is one of the garden's horticultural marvels—maple trees that have been delicately grafted to display two distinct foliage hues: green and red.

Emperor Gomizuno's (1596–1680) plan for this retreat drew inspiration from the gardens of the aristocrats of the Heian era (9th–12th centuries), who oversaw some of the world's finest landscape art. During that time, gardens incorporated references from geomancy, Confucianism, and religion.

Geomancy is reflected in *feng shui*, the spiritually determined placement of elements such as rocks, ponds, and the direction of streams. Confucianism introduced the opposing forces of *yin* and *yang,* dark and light, feminine and masculine. And Buddhism employed rock groupings to represent the legendary mountains mentioned in Chinese cosmology.

Shugaku-in's earliest inhabitants modeled their creations on those of the continent, but over time, incorporated native flowers and scenery as well as the demands of local climate and geography. With its steep

mountains, waterfalls, volcanoes, and lengthy coastline, Japan has some of the world's most beautiful and dramatic scenery. The natural phenomena that shaped these isles are reflected in the estates of the nobles.

Shugaku-in Imperial Villa employs three main gardening techniques. Exemplifying hide-and-reveal *(miegakure),* the lower grounds are traversed by paths that wind gently to ease the walk and reveal new features around each bend. Several notable stone lanterns catch the eye, including a Korean lantern said to resemble a kimono sleeve or a crocodile jaw. Seasonal plantings, uniquely-shaped trees, and attractive rock groupings delight the stroller. A canopy of trees that filters the sunlight adds to the feeling of a supremely natural and unrestricted setting.

Above Bamboo is sliced to make rakes while its bundled stalks form hand brooms for delicate caretaking.

Opposite above Morning light dapples a sinuous path.

Far left The shallow pond cooled imperial residents and augmented the scenery.

Left Stone stairs tucked into a mossy slope lead to the upper garden.

The second technique is asymmetry. Japanese gardens and homes are often designed on an asymmetrical axis, so that at first, as with Shugaku-in's teahouse, just a hint of a structure comes into sight. The whole is revealed in stages that encourage appreciation.

Lastly, is borrowed scenery *(shakkei),* and Shugaku-in presents one of the most dramatic uses of this technique that integrates the garden's natural backdrop. In the upper garden, tall hedges limit the view as the visitor enters a small, thatched gate. The feeling is of enclosure rather than restriction. At the uppermost teahouse, the scene bursts open to include the lake below and mountains beyond. It is a spectacular vision, enhanced by blooming cherry trees in spring, by vivid scarlet and golden maples in fall, and by the crystal beauty of a snow-covered landscape in winter. The lake adds refreshing breezes, while its reflection of the sky adds drama.

SANZEN-IN TEMPLE GARDEN

In former times, a day-long journey through a narrow, mountain pass along the Takano River was the only approach from Kyoto to Ohara. The village's farmers, woodcutters, and charcoal makers supplied the city's temples with food, lumber, and fuel.

Shaded by the Eastern Mountains, Ohara is just elevated enough to be a bit cooler than central Kyoto. The hushed, mountain-shadowed setting drew pupils from Enryaku-ji, the Tendai temple atop Mt. Hiei, to descend the mountain to study Buddhist chanting.

The main garden in Sanzen-in houses Ojo-gokuraku-in (Temple of Rebirth in Paradise). It was established during the 9th century—a time of expansion for the Pure Land sect, which saw Amida Buddha as its principle religious figure. The garden, a replica of the Pure Land in landscape, was a symbolic refuge for those waiting to enter paradise and to escape the endless cycles of rebirth.

The setting is majestically simple and calm. Cushions of luxurious moss are shaded by a leafy canopy of maples, under a growth of perfectly vertical cryptomeria trees. The contrast in greens, especially when the afternoon sun illuminates the foliage, is quite ethereal. Visitors may stroll through the grounds to view the figure, sculpted in 986, of Amida with two kneeling attendants, Seishi and Kannon. The setting is uncomplicated and ultimately restful—an appropriate manifestation of heaven on earth.

Below left The Suzaku-mon entrance for imperial guests glows with reflected light.

Below middle The lower garden is intended for viewing, not strolling.

Below Stately grove of tall cryptomeria trees interspersed with shorter maples shade the moss groundcover.

Left Tree frogs perched on a bamboo water spout blend into the garden greenery.

Far left Sweeping boughs spread their display of color.

Above Early morning rays of sun radiate through the forest.

Left Impressive cherry trees can be found in the upper Jigen Garden.

Bottom left Bamboo dippers shaped like snowshoes.

Bottom right Frost-glazed, newly fallen leaves.

Above left Snow hides and highlights shape and texture.

Above right Snow on the cedar shingle roof of the Buddha Hall.

Left Rocks placed with discerning care soften the sound of falling water.

HOSEN-IN TEMPLE GARDEN

Hosen-in is one of the subtemples at the foot of Mt. Hiei in Ohara where monks from the Tendai sect temple, Enryaku-ji, come to study Buddhist chanting.

The temple was partly rebuilt in the 17th century with timber from Fushimi Castle, after its warlord was defeated. Floor-boards stained with blood from

Opposite above The majestic trunk and limbs of a 700-year-old pine.

Opposite below A new garden to the east of the main hall.

Left A copse of thick bamboo sways behind the maples.

Left below Wisps of maple leaves on rocks, moss, and a cone of sand.

Below Steppingstones for cerebral, not physical passage.

Bottom Chinese bellflower offering before the Buddhist image of Fudo-myo.

battle were reverently made into a ceiling, so that no foot will ever tread them. In the main room of this teaching temple is a set of granite slivers that sound the pentatonic scale when struck. An earthen wall on the north side of the grounds is banked by a vivid, green copse of bamboo, beyond which are glimpses of the Ohara Valley.

Like the other nearby temples in this steep valley, Hosen-in exudes a feeling of isolation and serenity. Its garden features a unique, huge, and elegant seven-hundred-year-old white pine.

Pines were the first trees planted in ancient gardens, often when the designer wanted to evoke a shoreline or a scene from an ink brush painting. The tree is also used to symbolize pining for a person or a god,

Far left Whipped green tea and a sweet to warm the soul.

Left A dusting of snow crowns the peak.

Below A rocky shoreline brought inland.

Bottom, from left to right Rock-lined gravel border softened with moss displays the aesthetic principle of *wabi*. Not yet alight in the wind. Early-blooming sasanqua camellia placed on the moss-rimmed water basin.

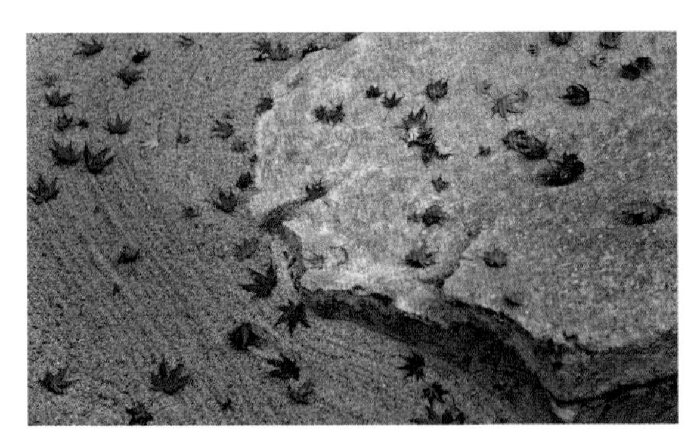

because the Japanese word for pine, *matsu*, is a homonym for waiting. And because the gods are believed to descend from pines to bring good fortune to those who harbor *matsu,* the trees bear spiritual meaning as well. Even today, at the New Year, people attach tiny pine seedlings—with needles, trunk, and roots—to house fronts to invite the goodwill of gods.

Whether or not Hosen-in's ancient pine hosts gods, it is certainly home to great beauty. Over centuries, as its magnificent limbs spread, the tree was supported to shape it into a work of art.

Right The majestic tree has respectful admirers.

Below Bracing air enhances a bowl of green tea and a snowy scene.

KAMIGAMO SHRINE GARDEN

Above Shrine-goers purify with water before paying respect to the gods.

Below The cone symbolizes the mountain peaks on which the Japanese gods descended.

One of the oldest Shinto shrines within the city proper, Kamigamo Shrine takes its name from the Kamo clan, which inhabited the area a millennium ago.

While Buddhism was imported from China, Shinto is Japan's native belief. Based on myth, it focuses on purity, fertility, and renewal. From ancient times, in recognition of the majesty of nature as a creation beyond human capability, shrines occupied sacred space *(yuniwa)*. Today *niwa* has taken on the general meaning of garden.

Shinto shrines begin with a twisted straw rope tied around a prominent boulder or giant cryptomeria cedar tree, or set before a waterfall. A surrounding area was cleared to mark a spiritual setting appropriate to approaching the gods and for prayer. Shrine buildings, added only after the 9th century, reflected native architecture, with raised floors supported by posts set directly in the ground.

A further demarcation was the *torii* gate: two vertical posts supporting two overhead horizontal beams. Beyond Kamigamo's large *torii* is a great expanse of open lawn. Families often gather there on weekends to picnic, but this space is also appropriated for entertaining the gods. Before festivals *(matsuri)*, shrine-goers purify themselves and then carry the *kami* (gods) around in a portable shrine. At Kamigamo, traditional horse racing and archery are held in this expanse twice a year, and Noh drama is performed in the roofed pavilion to further please the gods and ask their continued favor.

Just beyond the shrine entrance is a flat area of white sand broken by two conical mounds representing the mountain behind the shrine from which the gods descended. Each cone is topped with a

single pine *(matsu)* needle, *matsu* being a homonym for wait, in this case, for the gods.

Another sacred natural feature of shrines is a body of water, since the gods are believed to come from islands offshore. Additionally, the water fonts present at all shrines serve several spiritual purposes: They allow petitioners to purify themselves by rinsing their hands and mouth, and they

Above His prayers done, a silk-garbed Shinto priest leaves the shrine's main hall.

Right A covered bridge spans a slender stream that wends through the shrine precincts.

wash away illness or misfortune. Petitioners can also float their troubles away by writing prayers on paper that they place in a stream along Kamigamo's precinct's eastern border.

The shrine grounds are a form of sacred garden. Nothing may be taken from the area, and trees are neither cut nor planted. This natural environment is considered the gods' garden.

Kamigamo, Kyoto's northernmost major shrine, provides a quiet reserve of greenery punctuated with birdsong and the gentle sound of the stream winding its way through the grounds.

Above Shrine priests on their way to a ceremony; color denotes rank.

Right Mountains at the edge of the shrine are lush with greenery.

Below Sweeping a footpath at the edge of the vestigial primeval forest of the inner shrine.

Above, from left to right Candle-lit, lotus-patterned lanterns for a night event. Decorative prayer cylinders are left for the gods to enjoy. A twist of hanging straw denotes a sacred space

Below Several small family shrines line the hilly upper complex.

DAITOKU-JI TEMPLE GARDEN

This small Rinzai Zen temple was destroyed during the Onin Wars (1467–1477). But unlike Kyoto's other Zen temples, which flourished under the patronage of the shogun, Daitoku-ji was supported by the wealthy merchants of Sakai who funded its rebuilding.

It was here that drinking green powdered tea *(matcha),* became a popular pastime and a practice adopted by Daitoku-ji's abbot,

Ikkyu. Tea became an integral part of monastery life and eventually developed into a ritual or ceremony that was not only a form of discipline, but also a sophisticated entertainment. Although Daitoku-ji's main buildings retain the austerity proper to a Zen temple, the many subtemples preserve a variety of garden styles that encompass the dictates of both tea and Zen.

The 15th century was a period of political instability. The samurai military who moved the capital to Kamakura, near Tokyo, were drawn to the discipline demanded by the newly arrived Buddhist sect, Zen.

On leaving secular life, many of them became Zen monks, forsaking the pleasures of the world: reputation, food, wealth, sexual pleasure, even sleep. This rejection extended to their gardens. Bereft of showy plantings, these small, confined gardens expressed disregard for the symbols of wealth. Although Zen gardens do not require buying and maintaining exotic plants, Zen's dry, *karesansui* aesthetic requires much care. Acolytes are tasked with weeding and with raking the sand into patterns intended to trigger inner thoughts and to create a setting that directs the novice toward enlightenment.

Opposite Moss lapping at a sea of sand in Zuiho-in.

Above left Many shades of green on the approach to Koto-in.

Above right Rocky isles emerge through waves at Zuiho-in.

Above The narrow, maple-lined approach to Koto-in.

Left Cusped window in Korin-in.

Below, from left to right A circle of sand: hollow or hallowed? Black, twine-bound stone denotes no entry. Every raked line is intentional. Fan-shaped garden edge in Obai-in. Waves of sand focus the eye on a solitary rock.

Above left Undisturbed for centuries: an ancient maple in Koto-in.

Above right Purposely unpapered midsection of window panel at Obai-in.

Right, from top to bottom
Cascading branches of Japanese beautyberry (*murasakishikibu*). Rain-wet walkway. The beauty of stone enhanced by a simple fern. Wave upon wave.

The tea garden, on the other hand, serves as a passageway from the mundane to the profound world of tea.

Rather than a visual delight, it acts as an approach, a cleansing of the spirit, and a brief forsaking of the world. Flowers considered too showy or fragrant will not be planted. Moss is the preferred groundcover. And the path to a tearoom is often made of inset steppingstones, laid unevenly so that the guest must look downward when approaching—before looking up to enter into the world of tea.

Because they are still in active use, a number of Daitoku-ji's fine tea gardens can only be viewed from temple verandas—unless one is fortunate enough to be invited to a tea ceremony.

Daitoku-ji is highly regarded for its dry gardens, and the best known is in the subtemple of Daisen-in. The front garden is a vast, flat area of raked sand with groupings of rocks against the earthen wall. But it is the narrow side garden with its massive jutting rocks and raked sand that draws the most attention. The artist Soami is said to have based this tableau on Sung Dynasty painting, and visitors who rest their eyes on the rock placement can appreciate the resemblance to the rough, jagged strokes of an ink brush. Much of the temple's literature explains the Zen symbolism embodied within this narrow space, particularly the boat-shaped rock that "sails" on the dry stream toward the sea of eternal repose.

The subtemple Koto-in has a rare Zen garden. Rather than the usual dry landscape of stone and sand, it features a smooth, flat carpet of verdant moss, mottled by sunlight filtered through slender, hovering maples. Koto-in offers visitors a verdant break from the challenging discipline of controlled austerity.

Above A visitor holds a lacquered paper and bamboo umbrella at Korin-in.

Right A Zen principle codified in sand, rock, and moss in the Ryogen-in garden.

Opposite above Ryogen-in's smallest dry sand and rock garden.

Above left Rock placement is essential to the spatial elements of a Zen garden.

Above right Winter sun casts its long shadow at Daisen-in.

Left Koto-in is an unusual Zen garden, not of sand and rock, but of moss and maple.

Below The Jizozuka courtyard is filled with sacred Buddhist statuary of Jizo, a beloved Japanese guardian deity.

Bottom Fallen leaves decorate an historic stone basin in the stroll-garden of Koto-in.

JISSO-IN IMPERIAL GARDEN

Set near Kyoto's northern foothills is the ancient imperial temple and garden of Jisso-in. The temple was moved to this northern suburb of Iwakura in the 15th century. The present structure, built in 1709, is the oldest of its kind in Japan.

Known for its cool summers and frigid winters, Iwakura remained a detached and overlooked rural area until a new subway line linked it to the city in the 1990s. Today, much new housing has brought younger families into the agricultural community, still crisscrossed with traditional farmhouses and vegetable patches.

Jisso-in retains its elegant isolation and draws relatively few visitors, except in November when the maples shading the temple's entire north side transform the scene into shades of glorious crimson. The sharp decline in night temperatures promotes an abundance of brilliant autumn foliage.

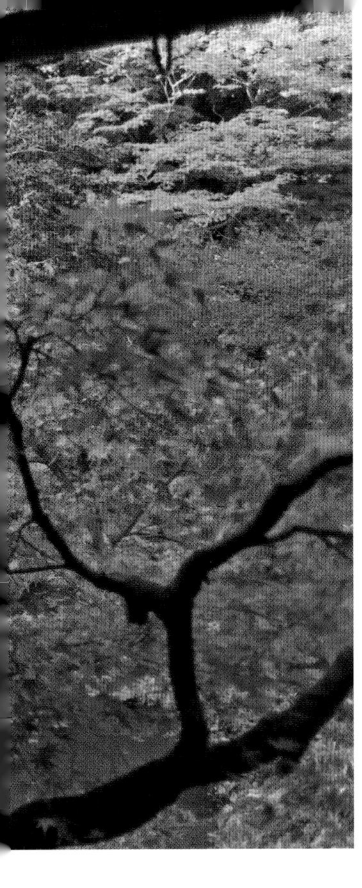

Opposite below Welcoming another day of appreciative visitors.

Above The ancient back garden noted for its pond and maples.

Right Jisso-in's cool, northern location fosters its luxurious moss and vivid maples.

The temple itself is best known for its unusual lacquered floor. Some fifty years ago, the resident priest removed the *tatami* mats that covered the floor. The dark floorboards were then lacquered

Left Echoes of the tsunami: steel arcs of incoming waves in the east-facing garden.

Below left A female blue rock thrush surveys the garden environs.

Below Shikyakumon Gate reveals a russet tableau within.

Right Slabs of rock span the ancient pond; a bridge as spiritual passage.

Far right Slow drops of water turn into gentle ripples.

Below right Behold, a *shidarezakura* weeping cherry tree at its peak.

so that they reflected the spectral beauty of the surrounding maples. In spring and summer the humble room glows with greens, and in autumn the glossy floor captures the fiery yellow, orange, and reds of the turning foliage.

The back garden dates from the medieval age, and its stone lantern and rocks reflect this antiquity. A large rectangular rock and three smaller boulders form a bridge across a pond lined with Japanese andromeda, coral ardisia, and leather fern. A reflective blush of flowering begonias colors the water in the square basin near the tearoom, and lusciously red clusters of berries on heavenly bamboo *(nanten)* announce their presence on snowy days.

The front garden, with its weeping cherry set in a medallion of moss and its arched stone sculptures, is a work in progress. Recently, a consortium of gardeners came from all over Japan to complete a reminder of the earthquakes that shook the ground and the tsunami that surged inland in 1995 and 2011. Steel arcs represent the waves, while a long mound of moss recalls the vulnerable land.

In an example of *shakkei* (borrowed scenery), Mt. Hiei looms over this suburb, fusing with and at times dominating the garden view.

Western Kyoto
500m
1500ft
N
Sekisui-in
Hachimangu Shrine
Saimyo-ji
Dongyo-ji
Jingo-ji
Kiyotaki Daigongen
Takao Village
Isho-ji
Arashiyama Takao Parkway
Shobudani-ike Pond
Shuzan Kaido
Mt. Sawayama 516m
Sowanoike Pond
Mt. Momoyama 460m
Koetsu-ji
Mt. Washiga-mine
Okitayama
Haradani Cherry Garden
Hidari-dai
Mt. Daimonji-yama
Kinugasa
Kyoko-chi
Domoto Museum
Mt. Kinugasa
Ryoan-ji Temple
Sampo-ji
Umegahata
Saiju-ji
Jikishi-an
Yomeibunko
Ritsumeikan University
Narutaki
Ninna-ji
Kitasaga
Ryoanji
Toji-in Temple
Fukuoji Shrine
Daikaku-ji Temple
Torii-gata
Osawanoike Pond
Utano
Ryoanji
Toji-in
Hirosawaike Pond
Adashino Nembutsu-ji
Yamagoe
Omuro Ninna-ji
Myoshin-ji
Gio-ji
Seiryo-ji
Narutaki
Keifuku Kitano Line
Keishun-in
Prefectural Gymnasium
Myoshin-ji Temple
Takiguchi-dera
Hensho-ji
Hanazono
Taizo-in
Hokyo-in
Nison-in
Rakushisha
Marutamachi-dori
Hokongo-in Temple
Jojakko-ji
Tokiwa
Hoju-ji
Arashiyama
Saga Arashiyama
Ogurayama Tunnel
Okochi Sanso
Torokko Arashiyama
JR Sagano Line
Hanazono
Uzumasa
Hanazono University
Randensaga
Rokuo-in
Kurumazaki
Toei Movie Land
Daihikaku
Tenryu-ji Temple
Arisugawa
Koryu-ji
Kurumazaki Shrine
Arashiyama
Ranzan
Katabira-no-tsuji
Ukyo Ward Office
Uzumasa-Yasui
Tenjin R.
Katsura River
Kyoto Saga University of Art
Shochiku Movie Studio
Uzumasa-Koryuji
Kaiko-no-yashiro
Sagano
Uzumasa
Uzumasa Tenjingawa
Nishioji
Horin-ji
Arashiyama
Arisugawa River
Yamanouchi
Sanjo-dori
Keifuku Arashiyama Line
Iwatayama Monkey Park
Mitsibishi Motors
Kyoto University of Foreign Studies
Umenomiya Taisha
Shijo-dori

CHAPTER 3

Gardens of Western Kyoto

Geomancy set the city limits, but nature—in the form of frequent flooding that ruined crops and destroyed dwellings—also imposed boundaries at Kyoto's western borders. Even today, this part of Kyoto retains a rural feel, with its small vegetable plots scattered around old aristocratic estates, Shinto shrines, and Buddhist temples.

Exempt from the confines of the original city plan, gardens within these temples are large. The land, however, is subject to the dictates of the Oi River that rushes through a steep gorge past the verdant hillsides of Mt. Arashiyama (Storm Mountain). Some of the city's most glorious views of seasonal flora draw photographers, artists, and tourists who crowd the streets as they take in the loveliness on foot or from picturesque rickshaws.

Clockwise from top left A rose pink lotus blooms at Hokongo-in. A thousand-year-old estate pond at Ryoan-ji. Listening for answers at Ryoan-ji rock garden. The pavilion and its reflected image, unrivaled among Kyoto's scenic spots. Stone *tsukubai* water basin for the tea room at Ryoan-ji.

KINKAKU-JI ESTATE GARDEN

This ancient estate, now a Rinzai-sect Zen temple, once belonged to the Heian period aristocrat Saionji Kintsune. Most visitors focus on the gold-roofed pavilion, but equally alluring are the grounds, an excellent example of 12th century gardening art.

When Shogun Ashigaka Yoshimitsu (1358–1409) acquired this property, the court was enthralled by 10th–13th century Chinese Sung Dynasty aesthetics. Yoshimitsu had the power and taste to replicate the ornate continental style when renovating his new palace complex. The garden, its pond, isles, rock groupings, and large plantings all complemented the architecture to produce one of Kyoto's most enduring examples of estate landscape.

By the 10th and 11th centuries, the imperial court was well established as a place to pursue scholarly and secular pleasures. Landscapers used the gardens of the previous capital, Nara, as a template. But as their skills, tools, and knowledge developed, they incorporated themes and styles from Chinese classics and painting. The 11th century book, *Sakuteiki*, lays out precise and sophisticated principles for this merged garden design. The attention to detail—from rock placement to river flow, from pathways to seasonal plantings—reveals much of the gardener's art and the householders' expectations.

The aristocracy displayed its erudition, aesthetic sensitivity, and appreciation of nature by incorporating scenes referencing literature and religious symbolism into its large gardens. Nor did the nobles neglect entertainments. Their residences included a flat area for games, sporting events, and poetry reading.

Murasaki Shikibu's 11th century novel, *The Tale of Genji*, provides many examples of the era's amorous diversions and poetic arts. The book also reveals how profoundly both men and women esteemed knowledge of flowers, fragrances, and color.

While ponds in Nara's gardens were designed for practical irrigation, in Kyoto's Heian period they became a central aesthetic component. By mirroring the surrounding foliage, they

Opposite above The approach beyond the tiled gate is a canopy of maple trees.

Opposite below A snow-capped Golden Pavilion is the visual holy grail for many Kyoto aficionados.

Right The pond's still surface mirrors the timeless architectural heritage.

Right above An isle of pine floats in the pond.

Above A lovely quartet promenade in *yukata* summer kimono.

Right Cotton clouds float above and below the radiant Golden Pavilion.

Below Fallen leaves and gnarled roots of a venerable maple.

enlarged the sense of space and provided residents a venue to float in flat-bottom boats to savor the scenery. Evoking a familiar theme in Chinese classic painting, the ponds often featured tiny islands that conjured famous off-shore isles or the jagged mountain hermitages of the immortals.

In our age of instant gratification, we can view a scene for a few minutes, snap a photo, share it immediately, and move on to another garden, the next diversion. It is easy for us, then, to lose sight of the great pleasure and time people of that ancient era took in recreating beautiful scenes to enrich and complement their lives.

Above An avalanche of snowy white cherry blossoms.

Left Upright rock as a Zen metaphor for a resilient carp fighting its way upstream.

RYOAN-JI ZEN GARDEN

Dry, nearly barren except for a few splashes of star moss, this garden has captured the attention of millions. Whether they admire it or are simply puzzled, few can resist a five-centuries-old allure that rests neither on the pleasure of strolling, nor on the beauty of seasonal blooms.

A Zen garden in its purest form, Ryoan-ji is a spiritual exercise for those who sit and contemplate the simple materials before them—materials as rich and deep as the religious doctrine they embody.

The lush, floral stroll gardens favored by Heian period aristocrats were products of a peaceful era. By the 15th century, when Ryoan-ji was built, struggles for power that had percolated for centuries exploded into the Onin war. Started in 1467, it lasted ten years, left the court and its attendant life in disarray, and reduced Kyoto to rubble.

The ascendant warrior class shunned expansive and conspicuous properties. Its leaders exchanged the court's fascination with gorgeous silk robes and perfumed sleeves for the cold rigors of martial arts and spartan living.

Austerity, however, did not mean eschewing the arts, but rather incorporating them into daily discipline. Zen played a great role, with its emphasis on mastering both mind and body, and living in the moment by attending to even the lowliest task with skill and care.

Gardens became smaller and more enclosed. Made from basic

Opposite above A garden with a timeless presence.

Opposite below In the tea garden, a water basin shaped like an ancient coin.

Right A task not lightly given nor lightly taken.

Above Learning to *see*.

Left Centuries of care, yet untouched by the ages.

natural materials, they were designed to imbue the viewer with a serenity that eased the cluttered mind and cleansed the spirit. The goal, then—whether in battle or in sweeping a path—was a focused mind. Garden design emphasized, recognized, reflected, and aided the attainment of that state.

Zen abbots used the spare scenes before them as teaching aids. Gardens began to reflect abstract and metaphysical themes such as the vortex, the universe, or humanity's ephemeral nature.

The meaning of the fifteen rocks that form Ryoan-ji is mystery for the visitor to explore and ponder. The garden's depth of beauty, simplicity, and soothing nature, however, is as clear as it is eternal.

Above Vines of wisteria turn spring mountainsides lavender and white.

Above right Ponds in the Heian period were large enough for seasonal outings aboard shallow-bottomed boats.

Right The alluring fragrance of spring—pink and white azalea bushes and a wisteria arbor in full bloom.

Above Only the patina on the earthen wall allows time to mark its passage.

Right A covering of snow grants the rocks a brief escape from their sea-bound setting.

Far right Narrow paths transverse the estate garden and its myriad plantings.

TOJI-IN TEMPLE GARDEN

Above The inviting first look from the Shoin study.

Left Lush setting for the teahouse water basin.

This Renzai Zen temple combines styles not often seen in one complex. Ashikaga Takauji (1305–1358), the shogun who reestablished Kyoto as the capital after it had been moved to Kamakura, founded this temple in the 14th century. The third Ashikaga shogunate, Yoshimitsu, built the Golden Pavilion, and the eighth shogunate, Yoshimasa, built the Silver Pavilion.

Rather than simply reflecting the political world of their times, these warlords stood out as aesthetically gifted innovators. They sponsored a revival of the arts and reestablished Kyoto as a cultural and artistic center

renowned for Noh drama, painting, and garden design.

Takauji's spiritual advisor, the Zen priest Muso Soseki (1275–1351), designed two gardens conducive to meditating: Saiho-ji, the moss garden, and Tenryu-ji. Although later changes at Toji-in reduced visual evidence of Soseki's influence, the grounds still offer excellent examples of dry, tea, and stroll gardens that incorporate classical features.

Toji-in is just far enough from mainstream tourist attractions to ensure that sightseers are few and the atmosphere hushed. Visitors often buy a bowl of whipped powdered tea and a sweet, sit on the veranda, and view the garden—a wonderfully relaxing indulgence.

Masses of clipped azalea and camellia bushes line the edges of a pond, shaped in a classical garden conceit like the Chinese character *shin*, meaning heart or spirit. A low, stone bridge crosses to an island, representing Mt. Horai, a legendary mountain of the immortals in Chinese cosmology.

To the left, the eye sweeps upward to a thatched teahouse, Seirentei (Teahouse of Clear Rippling Waves), which overlooks the deftly sculpted grounds. Most of the garden remains a deep green throughout the year—compact, yet restful. Guests can borrow slippers and stroll the grounds under the shady canopy.

The garden in front of the abbot's quarters is an expanse of white sand, relieved with patches of lush moss and set with several massive boulders. It presents an austere contrast to the dense, dewy ambience of the tea and stroll gardens.

Top Teahouse of Clear Rippling Waves, with swells of Japanese andromeda, azalea, boxwood, and hydrangea climbing upward to maples and bamboo.

Above A refuge of green tranquility.

Left Outside this hall, slippers await those wishing to enter the garden.

Left Vivid color transforms the front garden of raked gravel, rock, and moss.

Below Beloved old trees are propped up, not removed; signs of great age, valued for its beauty.

Bottom Temples are galleries for landscape art.

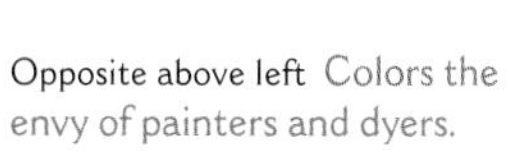

Opposite above left Colors the envy of painters and dyers.

Opposite below left A heart's desire: the stillness of the pond.

Left Slow, careful steps lead to the world of tea.

DAIKAKU-JI TEMPLE GARDEN

Daikaku-ji, in the city's far northwest, is a twenty-minute walk from Arashiyama's main tourist sights—and therein lies its appeal. Roadside stone pillars, set between large vegetable fields, mark the area as the late 9th century retreat of Emperor Saga.

On the grounds, Osawa Pond is a scaled-down version of China's Lake Dung Ting, after which it was modeled. Not only Kyoto's oldest constructed body of water, Osawa is the city's largest estate pond. Formed by damming the long-vanished Nakaso waterfall, it corrals the nearby mountain range into view and enhances the beauty of the Kyoto countryside.

For centuries, the most prominent feature in all ancient aristocratic gardens was a pond. It reflected the shimmering moonlight and shadowy mountains, cooled the residents with fresh breezes, and provided them with endless entertainment as they drifted across its placid surface to enjoy seasonal plantings from a maritime perspective. The reflection of the open sky gave a sense of quiet vastness, not found in the enclosed nature typical of most city gardens.

The pond recalls religious, literary, and cultural images. The recent addition of hundreds of lotus flowers complements the temple's spiritual environment. The smaller of its two islands—Chrysanthemum Isle, cited in the *Kokishu* anthology—evokes ancient poetry. And a series of jutting rocks that pierce the

Opposite The temple compound reflects the rural setting of this area of Kyoto.

Top An illuminated evening view of Shingyohoto Tower, a vermilion pagoda by Osawa Pond.

Above Covered boats ply the waters during autumnal full-moon festivities.

Left Saffron-robed Buddhist priests on their way to prayer.

Above Steep mountains shelter the city's northwestern edge.

Above right The complex consists of one-story halls linked by covered corridors.

water bear a picturesque resemblance to Chinese junks in a harbor.

Visitors are invited to partake in moon-viewing events by boarding dragon-shaped boats modeled on those raced across China's Dongting Lake. Today's guests, however, can enjoy their sojourn on the water at a more languorous pace.

The main temple buildings—constructed in the *shiden* (sleeping quarters) style of architecture—harken back centuries. Their raised, covered corridors span the numerous halls, where even the softest footfall causes the planks to emit a "chirp" resembling the sound of a bush warbler.

In one garden, medallions of moss set in an expanse of glittering white gravel provide a dramatic backdrop for treasured trees: a stately black pine or hanging cherry. The garden beside the vermilion-lacquered hall is filled with plantings to delight the eye, while a small waterfall adds pleasures for the ear.

The dry garden just north of the pond recalls the spirit of Nakaso Waterfall. Its silent cascade of rocks and gravel is a favored Zen conceit that reflects the sect's philosophy.

Above Early evening in a moss-covered inner garden.

Right above Bamboo skyscrapers.

Right below A border of glistening stones functions as a simple rain gutter beneath a roof eave in a courtyard garden.

Below Kyoto encourages nighttime events that spotlight the city's gorgeous fall foliage.

TENRYU-JI ZEN GARDEN

The 13th and 14th centuries were a time of superb landscape design. Perhaps the greatest master was Muso Soseki (1275–1351), a Zen priest who is credited with many of the gardens in western Kyoto, including Tenryu-ji. Muso was the first to consider the garden as a place for and an aid to meditation.

In the earlier Heian era, the grounds reportedly belonged to a prince and then, in 1270, became the residence of Emperor Gosaga. Today's visitors can enjoy the same views once enjoyed by imperial residents. Expanding the scene, covered passageways open onto fresh perspectives; paths wend along moss- and fern-covered hillside.

It is an extravagant setting with lush plantings and a pond filled with ever-expectant koi, that playfully disturb the placid surface in hope of forbidden hand-outs.

The pond also features a grouping of seven vertical stones. Their elongated reflections seem to reach into mist-enshrouded peaks. The scene

Opposite above An early morning task.

Opposite below A stream flows around the pavilion, cooling summer residents.

Above Transcending this world by crossing a bridge—a well-known Zen concept used in gardens.

Left The hillside is integrated into the view.

Right Clad in indigo robes, white leg wrappings, and straw sandals, Zen monks approach the main hall.

evokes the homes of the immortals, pictured in the Sung Dynasty ink brush paintings that provided inspiration.

Other, lower rocks draw the eye to focus on that vertical grouping, while incorporating views of Mt. Kameyama and Mt. Arashiyama. The dramatic blend of foreground and background creates the gardening conceit *shakkei* (borrowed scenery).

Most of the city's other Zen temple complexes were built in eastern Kyoto and were partially or wholly destroyed by frequent warfare. When rebuilt, they featured the new, dry gardens for which Zen is now popularly known. But Tenryu-ji, which precedes this era of reconstruction, is seen as a bridge spanning the 10th to 12th century stroll-type gardens and 14th century orthodox Zen gardens.

Minor changes have made the grounds more accessible to visitors, but Tenryu-ji remains one of Kyoto's oldest and most historic gardens.

Above left Raking the garden in the early morning hours.

Above right The gardener's presence is everywhere.

Left A boat-shaped rock as metaphor for passage to enlightenment.

Above Path through the mossy ground of Hogon-in.

Right Low, trimmed maples drape their boughs, like crimson robes, over the pond.

Left, clockwise from top left Soundless ripples. A clutch of ferns in a rocky grasp. Embedded border of round, roof-end tiles. The overhead canopy.

Below Symmetry in design as arresting as the contrast in color.

MYOSHIN-JI ZEN GARDEN

Kyoto's Zen temples were built, as in China, on a north/south axis, with the gate to the south and halls in a line reaching to the abbot's quarters. The layout in all Kyoto's seven Zen temples is identical. However as more land was acquired, new subtemples showcased elegant examples of domestic architecture and landscapes.

At Myoshin-ji, as with Daitoku-ji, Shokoku-ji, Tenryu-ji, Tofuku-ji and Nanzen-ji, subtemples that house active monasteries are closed to the public except on special occasions. Some of the open subtemples, however, occasionally serve powdered green tea *(matcha)*, and hold exhibitions, with the gardens providing an exquisite backdrop.

Taizo-in is one of the most famous gardens. Rather than the more common flat, dry surface of raked sand, it cascades down a slope to the viewing area. It is an innovative interpretation of an ink brush painting of a mountainside,

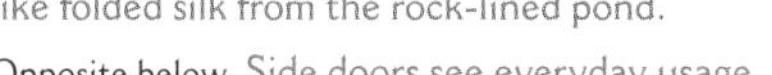

Opposite above Waves of greenery at Taizo-in rise like folded silk from the rock-lined pond.

Opposite below Side doors see everyday usage.

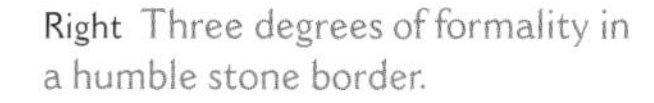

Right Three degrees of formality in a humble stone border.

Left The sliding doors are removed for expected visitors at Keishun-in.

Below Tidying the grounds, a resident monk carries a bundle of pampas grass.

Bottom Reed screens as sunshades are ubiquitous, and here, act as a foil to the autumn colors beyond.

rough with rocky cliffs and parted by a stream that courses downward until it widens and comes to rest in pools around flatter, broader stones at its base. The scene brings to life a painting usually associated with the Kano School of art, and indeed, one of this school's artists, Kano Motonobu (1475–1559), lived here.

The first and most important element in laying out the garden is the placement of rocks. They determine the flow of the stream, dry or liquid; direct the eye; and serve as religious symbols and icons. In Taizo-in the rock placement is masterly—an excellent example of Japan's aesthetic relation to stone.

Designing shrubbery and trees follows rock placement. In spring, the sculpted azaleas set Taizo-in's slope ablaze with color,

Above Tea, available to guests in many temples, prolongs a pleasurable visit.

Right White gravel waves swirl along a shore of moss and rock in the Zen garden at 15th century Daishin-in.

and provide deep contrast to the white sand. While this Zen garden departs from the typical spare use of material and severe linear format, it remains faithful to the sect's tenets.

Here, the viewer can sit before a compacted universe—a spiritual means of contemplation. The day-to-day care of this garden is the responsibility of Zen acolytes who rise before dawn. After morning prayers and meditation, they continue their religious practice though cleaning, weeding, and re-raking sections of sand.

Above An unusually long boxwood and azalea hedge at Keishun-in.

Left Monks returning from garden clean-up duties march past the Hatto Dharma Hall.

Right Star moss among the stones.

Far right Nerve bundle of red pine branches.

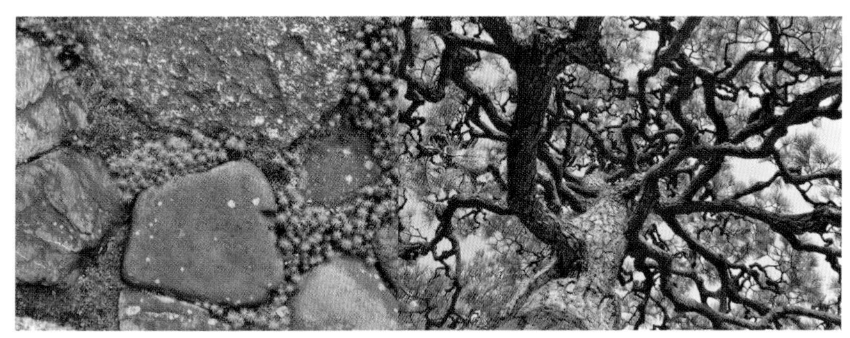

HOKONGO-IN VILLA GARDEN

Kyoto, the ancient capital, was divided into Right and Left Ministries in accordance with the principle of *yin/ yang*. Hokongo-in was originally the 9th century villa of the minister of the Right—equivalent to a prime minister. After his death, the villa declined. It was restored in 1129 and became a family temple for the Ashikaga shoganate in 1341. Centuries later, in 1937, when Marutamachi Street was widened, the grounds were reduced, and some of the buildings moved.

Although none of the gardens established twelve hundred years ago survived, historians know from literary descriptions and paintings that Hokongo-in retains some of its ancient landscape design features.

The garden's waterfall, set in the back, northeast corner, is purported to be the first of its kind in a Heian garden. Its flow was dictated by geomantic

Opposite above A refuge of serenity within a busy city.

Opposite below Daily scenery for the lucky locals.

Above Wayside Buddhist image.

Right The north section of the compound.

Below The pond surprises with multiple and unique seasonal viewpoints.

principles, as were the grounds, and indeed the city itself. Accordingly, Kyoto, like its Chinese predecessor, X'ian, was built on a north/south axis. Because Kyoto's north is thirty meters higher, the city's gentle incline facilitated pond construction and allowed streams to be designed with a propitious southwesterly flow.

Ponds also allowed the sophisticated residents to enjoy the craft and beauty aboard colorful boats, often to the accompaniment of music.

The stroll garden features a well-tended array of seasonal blooms: plum, cherry, iris, hydrangea, and water lilies as well as recently added varieties of potted lotus flowers that bloom through the summer.

These gardens linger as a testimony to the beauty of a peaceful and prosperous era. Their most prominent aesthetic principle is *miyabi*, a reverence for elegance expressed in one's esthetic refinement and reflected in every element of one's environment. *Miyabi* was expressed in the selection of fragrant incense individually mixed to reveal refinement, in the delicate dyes and designs on the twelve layers of silk robes worn by court women, in personal deportment, in a knowledge of poetry, in the ability to compose a clever or witty phrase, and in a sensitivity to the seasons.

Although an encroaching city has forced change—most visibly by placing a railroad along the villa's south side—Hokongo-in retains its *miyabi* character and its place as a fine example of Heian period elegance.

Left Originally a villa, the grounds were designed for strolling rather than contemplation.

Below An inedible, decorative fruit called the hand of Buddha.

Below middle An imminent bloom.

Bottom Enchi Pond is brimming with summer lotus plants.

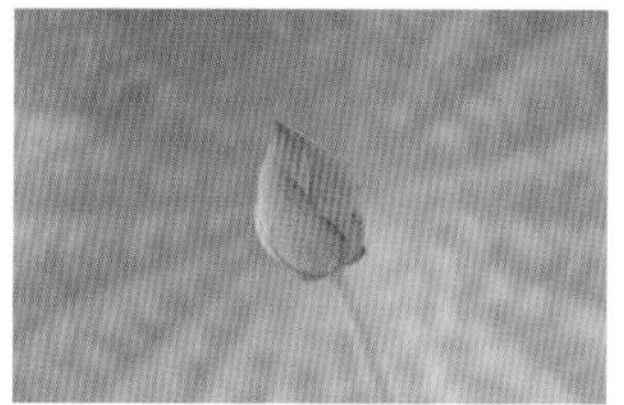

Opposite above An early morning visitor strives to compose flowering lotus in the Heian-era garden.

Opposite below The technique of gardening: a waterfall constructed a thousand years ago.

Below A close look at an exquisite pale pink *nelumbo nucifera*.

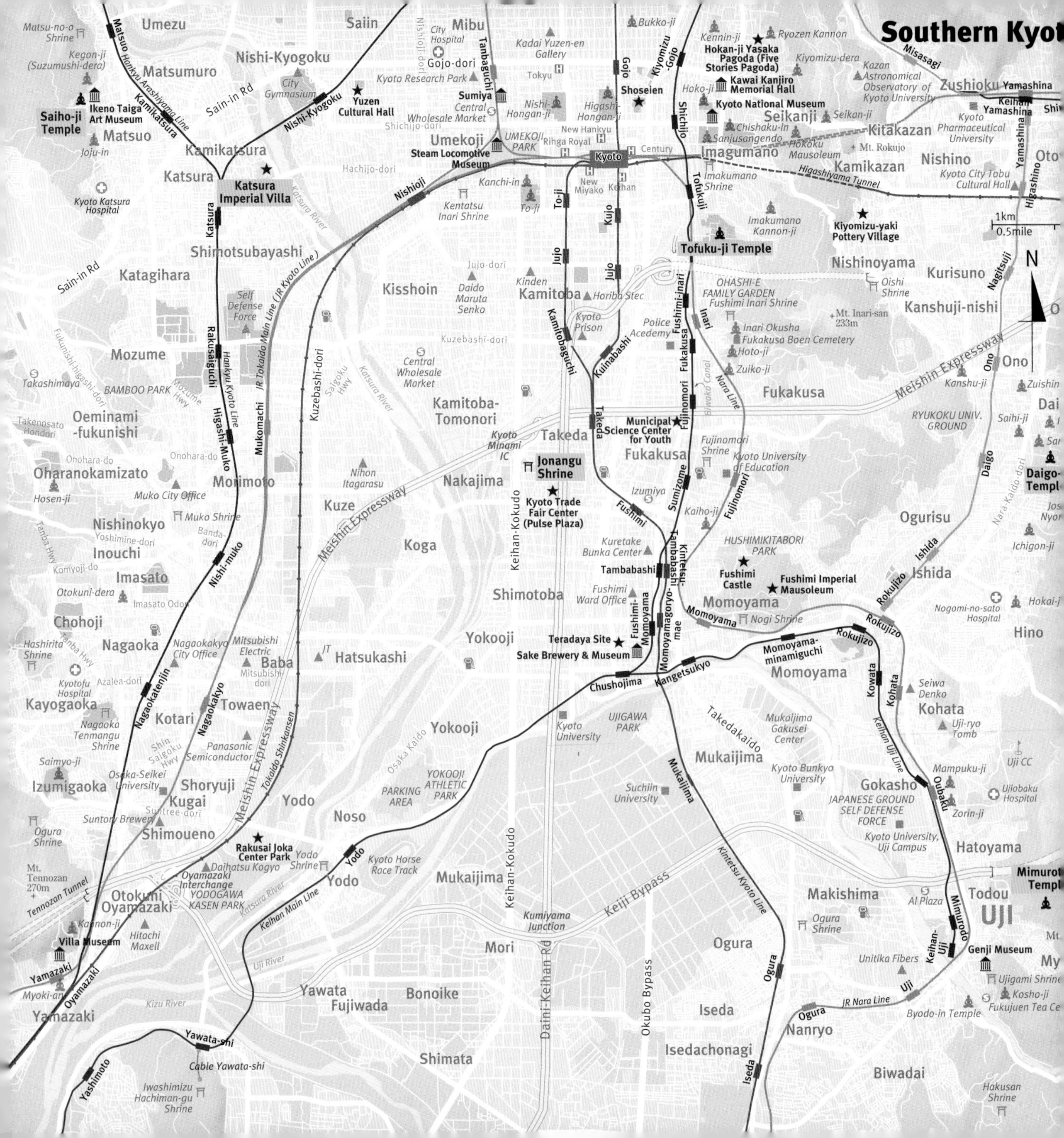
Southern Kyot
Matsu-no-o Shrine
Umezu
Saiin
Mibu
Bukko-ji
Kennin-ji
Ryozen Kannon
Hokan-ji Yasaka Pagoda (Five Stories Pagoda)
Kawai Kanjiro Memorial Hall
Kiyomizu-dera
Kazan Astronomical Observatory of Kyoto University
Misasagi
Zushioku
Yamashina
Keihan Yamashina
Kegon-ji (Suzumushi-dera)
Nishi-Kyogoku
Matsumuro
City Hospital
Gojo-dori
Kadai Yuzen-en Gallery
Kyoto Research Park
Tokyu
Gojo
Kiyomizu-Gojo
Shoseien
Hoko-ji
Kyoto National Museum
Seikanji
Seikan-ji
Kyoto Pharmaceutical University
Saiho-ji Temple
Ikeno Taiga Art Museum
Matsuo
Joju-in
Matsuo Hankyu Arashiyama Line
Kamikatsura
Sain-in Rd
City Gymnasium
Nishi-Kyogoku
Yuzen Cultural Hall
Sumiya
Central Wholesale Market
Shichijo-dori
Tanbaguchi
Nishi-Hongan-ji
Higashi-Hongan-ji
New Hankyu
Rihga Royal
Shichijo
Chishaku-in
Sanjusangendo
Hokoku Mausoleum
Kitakazan
Mt. Rokujo
Umekoji
Steam Locomotive Museum
Umekoji Park
Kyoto
Century
Imagumano
Nishino
Kyoto City Tobu Cultural Hall
Higashiyama Tunnel
Kamikazan
Katsura
Katsura Imperial Villa
Kyoto Katsura Hospital
Hachijo-dori
Nishioji
Kanchi-in
To-ji
New Miyako
Keihan
Kujo
Tofukuji
Imakumano Shrine
Imakumano Kannon-ji
Kiyomizu-yaki Pottery Village
1km
0.5mile
Kentatsu Inari Shrine
Katsura River
Shimotsubayashi
Tofuku-ji Temple
Jujo
Jujo-dori
Kinden
Horiba Stec
Nishinoyama
Oishi Shrine
Kurisuno
Nagitsuji
Sain-in Rd
Katagihara
JR Tokaido Main Line (JR Kyoto Line)
Kisshoin
Daido Maruta Senko
Kamitoba
Kyoto Prison
Kamitobaguchi
Kuinabashi
Police Acedemy
Fushimi-inari
Inari
OHASHI-E FAMILY GARDEN
Fushimi Inari Shrine
Mt. Inari-san 233m
Inari Okusha
Fukakusa Boen Cemetery
Hoto-ji
Zuiko-ji
Kanshuji-nishi
Kanshu-ji
Meishin Expressway
Ono
Zuishin
Self Defense Force
Rakusaiguchi
Mozume
Central Wholesale Market
Kuzebashi-dori
Saigoku Hwy
Katsura River
Fukakusa
Biwako Canal
Nara Line
Takashimaya
Bamboo Park
Mozume Hwy
Fukumishi-higashi-dori
Hankyu Kyoto Line
Mukomachi
Kuzebashi-dori
Kamitoba-Tomonori
Takeda
Fujinomori
Municipal Science Center for Youth
Ryukoku Univ. Ground
Dai
Saihi-ji
Takenosato Hondori
Oeminami -fukunishi
Higashi-Muko
Kyoto Minami IC
Takeda
Fukakusa
Fujinomori Shrine
Kyoto University of Education
Daigo
Nara-Kaido-dori
Daigo Templ
Onohara-do
Onohara-do
Oharanokamizato
Morimoto
Nihon Itagarasu
Jonangu Shrine
Nakajima
Izumiya
Sumizome
Hosen-ji
Muko City Office
Muko Shrine
Kuze
Kyoto Trade Fair Center (Pulse Plaza)
Fushimi
Kaiho-ji
Ogurisu
Nishinokyo
Yoshimine-dori
Banda-dori
Keihan-Kokudo
Kintetsu-Tambabashi
Hushimikitabori Park
Ichigon-ji
Inouchi
Tanba Hwy
Nishi-muko
Koga
Kuretake Bunka Center
Ishida
Komyoji-do
Tambabashi
Fushimi Castle
Fushimi Imperial Mausoleum
Imasato
Otokuni-dera
Imasato Odori
Shimotoba
Fushimi Ward Office
Momoyama
Rokujizo
Nogomi-no-sato Hospital
Hokai-ji
Chohoji
Momoyama
Nogi Shrine
Hino
Hashirita Shrine
Nagaoka
Nagaokakyo City Office
Mitsubishi Electric
Yokoji
Fushimi-Momoyama
Momoyamagoryo-mae
Momoyama-minamiguchi
Rokujizo
Tanba Hwy
Baba
Mitsubishi-dori
JT
Hatsukashi
Teradaya Site
Sake Brewery & Museum
Kyotofu Hospital
Azalea-dori
Chushojima
Kangetsukyo
Momoyama
Kowata
Kohata
Seiwa Denko
Kayogaoka
Nagaokatenjin
Nagaokakyo
Towaen
Kyoto University
Ujigawa Park
Takedakaido
Mukaijima Gakusei Center
Kohata
Nagaoka Tenmangu Shrine
Kotari
Yokooji
Keihan Uji Line
Uji-ryo Tomb
Shin Saigoku Hwy
Panasonic Semiconductor
Tokaido Shinkansen
Osaka Kaido
Mukaijima
Uji CC
Saimyo-ji
Osaka-Seikei University
Shoryuji
Yokooji Athletic Park
Mukaijima
Kyoto Bunkyo University
Mampuku-ji
Izumigaoka
Kugai
Parking Area
Suchiin University
Gokasho
Obaku
Ujiobaku Hospital
Suntory Brewery
Suntree-dori
Yodo
Noso
Japanese Ground Self Defense Force
Zorin-ji
Ogura Shrine
Shimoueno
Kyoto University, Uji Campus
Hatoyama
Rakusai Joka Center Park
Yodo Shrine
Yodo
Kyoto Horse Race Track
Keihan-Kokudo
Kintetsu Kyoto Line
Mt. Tennozan 270m
Daihatsu Kogyo
Oyamazaki Interchange
Yodogawa Kasen Park
Mimurot Templ
Tennozan Tunnel
Otokuni
Oyamazaki
Yodo
Mukaijima
Keiji Bypass
Makishima
Al Plaza
Todou
Katsura River
UJI
Kannon-ji
Hitachi Maxell
Keihan Main Line
Kumiyama Junction
Ogura Shrine
Mimurodo
Villa Museum
Mori
Ogura
Unitika Fibers
Keihan-Uji
Genji Museum
Mt.
My
Yamazaki
Uji River
Daini-Keihan Rd
Okubo Bypass
Ogura
Ujigami Shrine
Kosho-ji
Myoki-an
Oyamazaki
Yawata Fujiwada
Bonoike
Uji
JR Nara Line
Fukujuen Tea Ce
Byodo-in Temple
Yamazaki
Kizu River
Iseda
Ogura
Nanryo
Yawata-shi
Isedachonagi
Cable Yawata-shi
Shimata
Biwadai
Yashimoto
Iseda
Iwashimizu Hachiman-gu Shrine
Hakusan Shrine
N

CHAPTER 4

Gardens of Southern Kyoto

The mountains on the city's south soften into hills and then flatten where the Uji, Kamo, and Katsura Rivers converge on a plain that extends to Osaka and on to the Inland Sea. Barges filled with Kyoto's refined goods once floated downstream to the merchant city of Osaka and were pulled back to the capital by plough animals.

The river traffic is gone, but the area's farm women, some wearing indigo-dyed ikat *mompe* (baggy, cotton pants traditionally worn by farmers), still work the fields and sell their produce at outdoor stands.

Some temple gardens, set on nearby hills, incorporate enviable views of the city. Others, on flatter land, are famous for their enclosed and intimate settings. Jonangu, in particular, has great geomantic significance for Kyoto residents.

Clockwise from top left Round window, straight lattice doors, many shades of green beyond. A twin-like red pine with forked trunk and shapely limbs in the Rakusui-en sacred gardens at Jonan-gu. Saiho-ji's moss-softened bridge to the pond's isle. A visitor at Tofuku-ji. Japanese aesthetics dignify the ordinary, making it extraordinary.

SAIHO-JI MOSS GARDEN

The moist embrace of Kyoto's surrounding mountains brings long hours of shade that encourage a generous cover of thick moss. Overhead, bird songs resound through thickly forested hills.

Saiho-ji, originally an estate, became the first garden designed as an aid to meditation. This innovative, signature work by Muso Soseki (also Muso Kokushi, 1275–1351) changed Japan's concept of the form and function of landscaping, and radically altered the art of the garden. In this seemingly humble setting, Muso and his successors created a timeless masterpiece.

To maintain the reflective nature of the garden and its

Opposite above View of subterranean-like scenery from the pavilion's round window.

Opposite below A reliquary of Muso's spirit and a masterly understanding of natural beauty.

Above The breath of ancient earth.

Left Sprays of autumn color.

primeval natural beauty, the number of visitors is restricted. They must obtain advance permission and, on arrival, copy a sutra that the monks supply. Visitors are then free to wander around the grounds as they please.

Their first impression may be of having sunk into middle earth and emerged in a moist cavern—cool, removed, otherworldly. The twitter of coal tits, crows, and brown-eared bulbuls,

accompanied by the cooing of doves and the late-summer whirring of cicadas, accent the remote, ethereal atmosphere.

The grounds are laid out on several levels. Spidery maple limbs frame the entrance, setting the standard for the textured shades of green to come. The moss-lined path, speckled with fallen petals and leaves, leads down to and around a still pond. The air itself breathes antiquity.

Above left A garden repossessed by nature; none of the original plantings exists today.

Above right Soft mounds of moss rise upward: Saiho-ji boasts more than a hundred varieties.

Below Are there sufficient terms for all the shades of green?

The ground textures are so mesmerizing that visitors rarely look up at a forest of forty-meter-tall cryptomeria trees interlaced with maples. The oldest—a pair of four-hundred-year-old cryptomeria—and other plantings were not in Muso's plan. These dignified cedars bear witness to the steady renewal of new growth, even within such formal tradition.

This refuge of nature has been allowed the freedom to exist and evolve without the taming hand of humans. But at the same time, it is remarkable for the skill of the masterful gardener in drawing the visitor's focus from the magnificence that is overhead to the subtly gorgeous elements that lies at one's feet: more than one hundred varieties of moss. The unique perspective is the legacy of a sense of beauty reverenced by ancient Japanese and brought to life by its gardeners.

Top The still pond, its surface an opaque shade of green.

Above One variety of moss vying for attention.

Left A gardener sweeps near Saiho-ji's oldest tree—more than four hundred years old.

KATSURA IMPERIAL VILLA GARDEN

The epitome of tradition and ingenuity, and the culmination of centuries of gardening technique, Katsura Villa continues to astound.

The lines of the buildings and its surrounding landscape are simple yet refined, natural yet contrived. The defining principle is asymmetry, a design philosophy that marks Japan's faithful interpretation of nature. But the imperial villa's beauty is complex. Literary references and poetic finesse coordinate with and punctuate an array of aesthetic principles that govern the use of color, form, and graded levels of aesthetic formality as well as the conceits of hide-and-reveal *(miegakure) and* borrowed scenery *(shakkei).*

The residence was built for Prince Toshihito (1579–1629), and the garden created by Kobori Enshu (1579–1647), one

Opposite above The buildings and grounds embody the consummate vision of sophisticated simplicity.

Opposite below Moss-rimmed, arched bridge of earth, gravel, and wood.

Left Two degrees of formality in the paths of gravel: irregular inset stone and long rectangular lengths of granite.

Right above Veteran gardeners skillfully prepare decorative winter straw wrappings to protect subtropical palms from frost.

Right below Detail of a semi-formal rock and stone path.

Below Scenes from literature and locations famed for their beauty are main components.

of Japan's foremost landscape artists. For centuries the nobility would revere and adhere to his template and palette.

But it wasn't until 1930 that the spatial qualities of Japanese architecture became well known abroad. Architects and garden designers around the world praised and emulated the openness and modular format of the rooms. The particularly Japanese integration of garden

with interior space became a feature of private and imperial homes alike, although on quite different scales.

Katsura's main buildings sit on an asymmetrical axis, allowing visitors within and those approaching from the outside a variety of views and impressions. Paths laid with irregularly shaped stepping-stones placed at unequal distances force strollers to stop and behold scenes along the way: a reference to classical literature, a select rock grouping, a seasonal planting, a glimpse of the raised buildings.

Shin-gyo-so concepts (formal, semi-formal, informal) appear in the use of the stonework and plantings. The stately pine, for example, is considered *shin*, azalea bushes embody *gyo*, and the morning glory vine is *so*.

The designers incorporated this panoply of conceits and principles to trigger viewers' sentiments and memories, and to enhance their pure esthetic enjoyment.

Set in southwestern Kyoto, Katsura, and the river that shares its name, is now a ten-minute train ride from the city center. It is one of the three imperial villas that require permission to enter. It is hoped that limiting visitors will lessen the risk of deterioration and help preserve the serene atmosphere integral to the landscape.

The fruition of centuries of superb gardening technique and a living embodiment of a vast knowledge of literature, Katsura melds the beauty of nature with the skilled, human hand.

Above Katsura—regarded as the perfect blend of architecture and horticultural art.

Far left A pair of visitors, male and female mandarin ducks.

Left Immutable stone lantern and ephemeral autumn maple.

Above left The camera flashes, another moment celebrated.

Above right The rusticity of the mossy thatched roof and highly sculpted pines in horticultural and architectural balance.

Left A hearth, shelves, and cabinet for the practice of tea.

JONANGU SHRINE GARDEN

Japan's earliest gardens were dictated by geomancy, taboo, geography, and poetry. Jonangu is a composite of all these principles, revealed through the gardener's hand.

Kyoto is protected on three sides by a natural barrier of mountains, but open on the south to invading forces. City planners, wanting a shield against danger, turned to myth and symbol. A line drawn south from ancient central street Suzaku-oji (now Senbon-dori) reached Okura Pond, representing the Crimson Phoenix. The other cardinal directions were similarly guarded: The east was protected by the Blue Dragon in the form of the Kamo River; the north by Mt. Funaoka, represented by the Black Turtle; and the west by the Konoshima-oji Canal, embodying the White Tiger. With these gods in place, the planners declared the city safe and in balance with the principles of geomancy.

Most estate gardeners acknowledged these beliefs. Planners were encouraged to create landscapes in accordance with a complex set of positive and negative dictates. If, for example, a stream did not flow in the propitious southwesterly direction, it would bring ill health. Conversely, an expanse of white sand was auspicious, since it purified the place where petitioners appealed to the sacred, native gods.

Jonangu is a repository of these ancient superstitions and principles. Many Kyoto citizens still seek good fortune when purchasing a home by buying an amulet at this Shinto shrine and installing it in their new dwelling. And indeed, the large parking lot and staff accommodate the hundreds of homeowners who visit the shrine year-round to request or renew a blessing.

Jonangu's other, newer attraction is its gardens, which represent three different periods: Heian, twelve hundred years ago; Muromachi, five hundred years ago; and modern day.

The Heian period replica is next to the entrance where tickets are sold. Its low mounds represent mountains in Chinese cosmology, and the streams that feed its pond flow auspiciously from northeast to southwest.

Opposite above One of the shrine's maidens mindfully sets down a bowl of tea.

Opposite below Sharp, vertical rocks pierce grassy mounds in this example of exuberant contemporary landscape.

Above A traditional tea garden viewed from within its teahouse.

Right Muromachi garden, designed by Nakane Kinsaku and modeled after those of four hundred years ago.

bridge. In this 16th century-style garden, space is more concentrated, and plantings around the rock-lined pond are compact and low. Visitors can drink tea in the teahouse and view the landscape from the perspective for which it was designed.

All three gardens are an inspiring testimony to Japan's continuing devotion to the art of the garden.

The mossy groundcover is rich with flowers mentioned in ancient texts. In the spring and autumn, people don period clothing and sit by the winding stream to read and compose poetry. Some beloved verses appear on fan-shaped signs along the stream.

Across the entry road is an open, contemporary area that uses modern material and techniques to interpret traditional gardens. Bordered by high, clipped hedges, it features a grass lawn interrupted by several rock groupings that are highlighted by a scattering of cycad palms among the sculpted azalea.

Around the teahouse is the Muromachi garden with its adjacent pond and low, stone

Opposite above Massive cycad palms, unseen in traditional gardens, bring an exotic appeal.

Opposite below Children visit the shrine for a special blessing on the occasion of *Shichi-go-san*.

Left A shrine priest's daily chore.

Right The grain of a wood plank contrasts stones set in a bed of gravel at the teahouse edge.

Below A brilliantly colored carp swims through a deep blue autumn sky.

MIMUROTO-JI PARADISE GARDEN

Uji, the ancient city to the southeast of Kyoto, is associated with *The Tale of Genji*, Lady Murasaki's novel of love and intrigue in the 11th century. But long before that time, aristocrats built villas and temples, including the renowned Byodo-in, along the cool and beautiful banks of the Uji River. The eponymous bridge that spans that river, built in 646, predates Kyoto.

The name Uji is also synonymous with the cultivation of the fine green

tea that flourishes in undulating rows in the moist air that envelops the town.

Most area temples are near the river, but Mimuroto-ji, tenth stop on the Thirty-three Goddess of Mercy Pilgrimage, lies among the hills, up a steep road.

The temple's 10th and 11th century gardens were termed "paradise gardens," because they attempted to reproduce Amida Buddha's heavenly home.

Today, Mimuroto-ji is also famous for its phenomenally lovely, flower-filled landscape. The azalea and rhododendron bushes that line the hillsides mingle with two-meter-high hydrangea, while more rhododendron fill the valleys below.

In 1989, scholar and garden designer Nakane Kinsaku turned these hillsides and vales into a vision of modern paradise with thousands of blooms.

Opposite above Early morning visitors.

Opposite below Designed by Nakane Kinsaku , the garden is fresh with dense plantings arranged around scenic rock groupings.

Above left Rhododendrons reach up the hillside.

Above right Rest pavilions for the many visitors are greatly appreciated, especially during the June rainy season.

Below White *nelumbo lutea* lotus grace the Hondo Hall's courtyard garden.

Myriad potted lotuses, a symbol of rebirth, are gathered immediately in front of Mimuroto-ji's Chinese-style main hall. In April, May, and June, all its flowering bushes engulf the mass of visitors in a luxurious display of color and provide a uniquely extravagant experience.

Numerous vendors outside and on the grounds offer samples of their fine, fresh tea, which visitors can enjoy while they sit and inhale the glorious fragrance of fresh azalea blossoms.

Opposite above The hillside anticipates a riot of color in early spring when thousands of rhododendrons burst into bloom.

Opposite below The hillside pathway, lined with massive boulders and trimmed pines, is as attractive in the distance as it is for those strolling among its plantings.

Below A pastel palette of azaleas and matching attire.

Above A canopy of pine boughs filters the sunlight.

Left The central garden is contained and compact.

Right Mimuroto-ji is the 10th temple in the Saigoku, Goddess of Mercy Pilgrimage.

DAIGO-JI TEMPLE GARDEN

Established in the 9th century by Rigen Daishi, the temple was named after then-Emperor Daigo. The large complex is divided into lower *(shimo)* and upper *(kami)* sections, and features Kyoto's oldest five-storied pagoda, erected in 951.

The subtemple, Sambo-in, is best known for its garden, created under the auspices of the 16th century warlord, Toyotomi Hideyoshi (1534–1582).

When he came to power, warfare had leveled most structures in central Kyoto. Daigo-ji, in a southeast section of the city, attracted Hideyoshi's special attention. His reconstruction efforts included planting hundreds of cherry trees, whose blooms provided a gorgeous setting for festivities.

An avid tea ceremony practitioner, he also sponsored massive ceremonies for the public and encouraged the development of tea utensils, tearooms, and tea gardens.

Then as now, the world of tea allows participants to transition from the mundane to the spiritual realm. The tea garden, devoid of showy or strongly scented flowers, typically avoids worldly distraction.

Approaching Daigo-ji's teahouse on steppingstones

Opposite above left The Sambo-in garden displays Hideyoshi's military strength and might, rather than serenity.

Opposite below Three quinces beside a water basin.

Above The pond is named for Benten, one of the seven lucky gods.

Left Seven hundred stones took decades to place.

leading through a low entrance, the visitor is forced to bow low. A humbling stance for warriors, this posture signals a pause in worldly matters, the irrelevance of titles, and the assumption of equality among all who enter the unpretentious room. Within the confines of the tiny hut, guests share the pleasure of drinking finely whisked, powdered tea from a simple bowl, while discussing the beauty of the restrained setting.

Hideyoshi, despite the tea ceremony's focus on humility, was fond of extravagant and rare items, and as due his station, received many gifts,

Above Sambo-in's outer stroll garden.

Right Fine, raked gravel spread in concentric circles gives birth to emerging rock isles.

including stones. Japanese have valued rocks and pebbles for centuries, believing that in addition to their beauty, they possess a spirit that imparts a special power. One resembles the jagged cliffs inhabited by the Chinese immortals or invokes a wind-slashed coast. Another stone, with a particular moss-lined cleft, recalls a mountain waterfall. In all gardens, while the choice and positioning of flowering bushes and trees may evolve over the ages, the initial rock placement is a permanent marker of the garden's legacy.

A rock grouping or an especially distinguished rock is designed to capture the eye and become the focal point of the setting. Sambo-in, however, defies this simple dictum. Seven

Top The horizontal pole indicates that visitors may look but not enter.

Above One of the pond's denizens.

Left Retainers bearing rocks traveled from all over the country to present them to the warlord Toyotomi Hideyoshi.

Below, from top to bottom The straw wrapping protects the pine against winter cold and invasion by climbing insects. Cherry blossoms rise above Sambo-in's wall. Considering himself on equal footing with the imperial family, Hideyoshi usurped the imperial crest for use on this gate. Maples against deep green foliage.

hundred rocks, mostly gifts to this powerful warlord, lie within the temple walls. They appear to some like a scattering of jewels, to others, a pretentious, discordant display of wealth. But in either case, the impression they leave is indelible.

The architecture of Sambo-in's main hall harkens back a thousand years to the *shinden* style (literally, sleeping quarters). *Shinden* features raised halls, which allow the wind to blow under the verandas and onto the rock-lined pond. Although the garden is only for viewing, the small, distinct bridges of logs, stone, and moss-covered earth invite the imagination to stroll and dream.

Below Hillside waterfalls above Bentendo Hall soothe the senses.

Bottom A thick growth of moss carpets the bridge.

TOFUKU-JI ZEN GARDEN

Resting along the southern peaks of the Eastern Mountains, this Zen temple retains the compact gardening style that the newly arrived Rinzai sect was developing in the 13th century.

Tofuku-ji has several notable gardens, but it is the brilliant

autumn maples, filling a ravine spanned by a covered wooden bridge, that command the attention and draw visitors. The temple compound presents a spacious, treeless contrast. Its inlaid stone paths lead to all the major halls. Its buildings lie on a symmetrical axis that reflects a Chinese geomantic principle.

Founded centuries ago, the *hojo* (abbot's quarters) was completely rebuilt in 1939. Its

Opposite above The covered bridge, Gaun-kyo, spans a steep maple-filled ravine.

Opposite below The landscape artist Mirei Shigemori favored vertical rather than horizontal stones.

Above Guided by ancient dictates, Shigemori's brilliant use of moss and stone becomes minimalistic art.

Right The grounds are famous for their mix of yellow and red maples.

Right *Karesansui*–a dry rock garden to stimulate the mind, not the senses.

Below Massive boulders in the front garden of the abbot's quarters echo the strength of Zen precepts.

20th century gardens are some of Japan's best examples of contemporary Zen-inspired landscape.

Mirei Shigemori's (1895–1975) concept for these technical and aesthetic masterpieces was to frame an austere Zen-style garden within a modern perspective. Traditionally, Japanese gardeners perfected the use of horizontally laid rock, while Chinese gardens favored vertical placement. Shigemori incorporated both. The south garden, acknowledging the influence of Chinese Sung Dynasty painting, contains massive vertical rock groupings that represent mountains. They contrast with horizontal stones set like islands in a sea of raked gravel. The effect is powerful, almost overwhelming—a challenge for the novice.

In the west garden, Shigemori sank small, granite squares into a soft bed of moss and deftly juxtaposed them with clipped azalea bushes set on a gravel groundcover to form a checkerboard pattern. The startling and pleasing effect of these three elements make this one of the most photographed gardens in Kyoto, rivaled in popular appeal only by Ryoan-ji and Daisen-in.

The grounds of the subtemple Fumon-in lie across a covered bridge that spans a narrow ravine and leads through a massive gate. Within a rectangular courtyard, the garden was sliced into two parts in the 19th century. The area on the right, featuring tortoise and crane imagery, is dense and compact, with masses of rocks interspaced with clipped shrubs. The left side is clean and spare, with raked sand and a single tree.

Funda-in, another subtemple, has a fine example of a classical raked-sand garden bordered with moss, clipped shrubbery, and trees. The simplicity of the raked pattern is refreshing and quietly appealing.

The gardens of Tofuku-ji weave centuries-old Zen design into our contemporary age, while keeping alive a visual perspective that continues to enrich the world of landscape gardening.

Above left Corridors connecting the one-story halls allow multiple views.

Above middle The teahouse garden of Funda-in.

Above right A cylindrical stone pillar used as garden ornament.

Right A covered bridge hovers above resplendent color.

Above The emerging head and wings of a dragon in Ryogin-an.

Right Sinuous, writhing dragons surge through clouds.

Far right Gently teasing away the winged seeds of the maples.

Below Fumon-in's garden is composed of dense groupings of moss, azalea, and blocks of stone.

From far left Forked-lightning design on the fence expresses a prayer for rain, essential in rice planting season. How simple and pleasing it appears. A well cover made of bamboo lengths lashed together by blackened straw rope. Geometric to a point, the garden edge.

Gardens Glossary

ajisai Hydrangea.

aware An aesthetic term for compassion or pathos when describing a deeply moving scene or work of literature.

Buddhism A religion originating in India and entering Japan via China in the 6th century.

cha-no-yu The art of the tea ceremony during which a guest is served a traditional sweet and then a bowl of whisked, powdered green tea.

chashitsu A tearoom or teahouse.

cho Districts within the city used as addresses.

cryptomeria A kind of Japanese cedar *(cryptomeria japonica).*

dai The Chinese character for big.

dodan tsutsuji An early-blooming azalea with clusters of tiny white flowers.

dori Street, as in Kawaramachi-dori.

engawa A low veranda.

enju Pagoda tree.

feng shui Literally, wind/water, the Chinese means of determining propitious directions.

geiko The preferred term for geisha in Kyoto.

hojo An abbot's quarters within a temple.

ikat A textile where the threads are dyed in patterns marked off by wax and then woven.

-in Denotes a subtemple.

-ji Denotes a temple.

jinja, taisha, jingu Shinto shrines.

kami Refers to the pantheon of Japanese gods, also "upper."

koan Spiritual conundrum given to Zen students.

karesansui A dry rock and sand garden found in many Zen temples.

kawa or –gawa River.

Kokinshu A 10th century anthology of poetry.

matsu Pine tree, also "to pine/wait for."

matsuri A festival honoring the gods.

matcha Powdered green tea.

miegakure Hide-and-reveal—the gardening concept that allows features to be discovered in stages.

mitsuba tsutsuji An early-blooming azalea.

miyabi An aesthetic term for playful elegance.

miyako The capital.

mompe Baggy, farmers' pants.

Namu Amida Butsu Honen taught that believers could attain salvation by chanting this invocation of Buddha's name.

nehanzu A picture of the reclining Buddha.

nenbutsu An invocation of gratitude to Buddha.

pagoda A multi-tiered structure within temple complexes for housing Buddhist relics.

sabi An aesthetic term referring to the aged beauty of an object.

satsuki Azalea.

sekimori-ishi A boundary stone set on a path to denote no passage.

shakkei Borrowed scenery—the gardening concept of including and incorporating scenery beyond the garden's proper border.

Sakuteiki An 11th century text explaining gardening techniques.

shakunage Rhododendron.

shibui An aesthetic term for understated, subdued elegance.

shimo Lower.

shin The Chinese character meaning heart or spirit.

shin-gyo-so Three levels of formality starting at the most formal.

shinden Raised halls for living and sleeping quarters favored since Heian period, twelve hundred years ago.

shinden-zukuri Literally, sleeping halls, an architectural style popular in the 9th century.

Shinto Native Japanese religion.

shogun Warlord.

shoganate A line of military leaders.

shoji A wooden lattice door or window covered with thin, almost transparent paper.

shrine A designated space for communing with the Shinto gods.

tatami Thick, rectangular mats woven of straw and used as floor covering

temple A structure for housing Buddhist images and holding Buddhist ceremonies.

torii A gate to a Shinto shrine, usually constructed of two horizontal posts and two vertical beams.

toro A stone lantern.

tsukubai A stone basin often seen in tea gardens.

tsuru-kame Paired crane and tortoise, an Asian symbol of longevity and immortality.

tsutsuji Azalea.

uguisu-bari The sound resembling a bush warbler that wood planks emit when trod on.

wabi An aesthetic term for beautiful rusticity.

yama Mountain.

yugen An aesthetic term for a mysterious beauty that evokes a profound feeling in the viewer.

yuniwa An open sacred space in which to approach the gods.

Zen Sect of Buddhism, another reading means good or virtuous.

Time Periods

Early Heian (794–894)
Late Heian (894–1185)
Kamakura (1185–1333)
Muromachi (Ashikaga) (1334–1573)
Momoyama (1573–1615)
Edo (1615–1868)
Meiji (1868–1912)
Taisho (1912–1926)
Showa (1926–1989)
Heisei (1989–

Bibliogaphy

Clancy, Judith, *Exploring Kyoto*, Stone Bridge Press, 2008

Keane, Marc P., *Japanese Garden Design*, Charles E. Tuttle, 1996

Keane, Marc P., *Songs in the Garden,* MKP Books, 2012

Kinoshita, June and Palevsky, Nicholas, *Gateway to Japan,* Kodansha, 1990

Mertz, Mechtild, *Wood and Traditional Woodwork in Japan,* Kaiseisha Press, 2011

Richie, Donald, *A Tractate on Japanese Aesthetics*, Stone Bridge Press, 2007

Takei, Jiro and Keane, Marc P., Sakuteiki, *Visions of the Japanese Garden,* Tuttle Publishing, 2001

Treb, Marc and Herman, Ron, *The Guide to the Gardens of Kyoto,* Shufunatomo, 1993

Below A migratory resident finds safe haven amidst cherry blossom reflections at Heian Jingu.

Acknowledgments

My greatest appreciation goes to all the gardeners who today continue to carry this centuries-old tradition of creating and maintaining some of the world's most beautiful landscapes. The world owes thanks to all who labor to reshape the land into a piece of beauty—from the early artists who created theory and design, to the humble many who stoop daily to gently nudge free a weed from the carpet of moss and who skillfully sculpt a shrub into an exquisite shape.

Marc Keane's book *Japanese Garden Design* is a masterful work that educates the reader about all the concepts that are integrated into a culture that has transformed this land as no other country has. His translation of *Sakuteiki* is essential to understanding the historical ideology behind Japanese gardens. I am most grateful to have his scholarship to refer to.

Terry J. Allen has lent her considerable editorial skills to bring precision and grace to abstract, aesthetic concepts. Her knowledge of Japanese culture complements her ability to glean and elucidate my thoughts and organize them into a most readable text.

I credit Allan Mandell with the phrase "the art of seeing" whereby the gardens become a guide to learning to understand the concepts of "emptiness within harmony."

June Chong is the editorial supervisor who very patiently and gently herded these chapters into an impressive whole.

Lastly, the inspired photography of Ben Simmons presents the eternal beauty of Kyoto, and infuses it with a power and presence that is as genuine this century as it has been for millennia past. His eye is unerring in teaching the viewer what and how to see.

JUDITH CLANCY

It has been my great pleasure and good fortune to collaborate with Judith Clancy and Eric Oey for this special project—Kyoto's gardens are a unique treasure of concentrated beauty and spirit found nowhere else.

For their kindest support and invaluable assistance, I am indebted to June Chong, Chan Sow Yun, Terry J. Allen, Yuichi Kurakami, Yuri and Takuji Yanagisawa, Isamu Nishida, Tomoyo Yasuda, Yoko Yamada, Shiro Nakane, Mira Locher, Julia Nolet, Teiko Seki, Katharine Markulin and Koichi Hama, Kate Klippensteen, Barry Lancet, Robert Hancock, Takeshi Setogawa, Don Morton, Rumiko Honma, Naoto Ogo, Atsuro Komaki, Tomoko Minami, Hiroshi Tanaka, Mechtild Mertz, Karin Swanson, Machi Horie, Miyuki Ikeda, Masanobu Kanda, Toshifumi Owa, Kathryn Gremley, Marvin Jensen, Kraipit Phanvut, Dennis Bones Carpenter, Will Taylor, Richard Cheatham, Sarah and Greg Moon, Deborah and Vince Collier, Rebecca and Joe Stockwell, George McCarten, Bill and Julie Hope, Kenji Sakai, Shaun Heffernan, Sarah Auman, Yuki Hashimoto, Karen and Stan Andersen, Evon Streetman, Jerry Uelsmann, Bill and Pat Crosby, Sandy and Gary Jobe, Jay Phyfer, Rieko Matsumoto, Florinda Angeles, Ryoko Tsujimura, Yukie Suzuki, Reina Ogawa, Sonny and Rie Satoh, Robert Kulesh, Lourie Travis, Hans Krüger, Noriko Yamaguchi, Kyoko Matsuda, Keiko Odani, Tatsuhiko and Rika Tanaka, Caroline Parsons, Pamela Pasti, Miwako Takagi, Thomas Ward, Wanrudee Buranakorn, Dom Giovannangeli, Kazuhiko Miki, Philip Rosenfeld, Ninomiya Takahashi, Fukuo Nagase, Natsuko Tanaka, Chiaki and Yoshihumi Nishida, and my friends at Myoren-ji. Heartfelt thanks to you all!

BEN SIMMONS/PHOTOGRAPHER

Published by Tuttle Publishing, an imprint of Periplus Editions (HK) Ltd

www.tuttlepublishing.com

ISBN: 978-4-8053-1596-5
(Previously published under ISBN 978-4-8053-1321-3)

Distributed by
North America, Latin America & Europe
Tuttle Publishing
364 Innovation Drive
North Clarendon, VT 05759-9436 U.S.A.
Tel: 1 (802) 773-8930; Fax: 1 (802) 773-6993
info@tuttlepublishing.com
www.tuttlepublishing.com

Japan
Tuttle Publishing
Yaekari Building 3rd Floor
5-4-12 Osaki Shinagawa-ku Tokyo 141-0032
Tel: (81) 3 5437-0171; Fax: (81) 3 5437-0755
sales@tuttle.co.jp; www.tuttle.co.jp

Asia Pacific
Berkeley Books Pte. Ltd.
3 Kallang Sector #04-01, Singapore 349278
Tel: (65) 6741-2178; Fax: (65) 6741-2179
inquiries@periplus.com.sg; www.tuttlepublishing.com

28 27 26 25 24 10 9 8 7 6 5 4 3 2 1

Printed in China 2403EP

"Books to Span the East and West"

Tuttle Publishing was founded in 1832 in the small New England town of Rutland, Vermont [USA]. Our core values remain as strong today as they were then—to publish best-in-class books which bring people together one page at a time. In 1948, we established a publishing outpost in Japan—and Tuttle is now a leader in publishing English-language books about the arts, languages and cultures of Asia. The world has become a much smaller place today and Asia's economic and cultural influence has grown. Yet the need for meaningful dialogue and information about this diverse region has never been greater. Over the past seven decades, Tuttle has published thousands of books on subjects ranging from martial arts and paper crafts to language learning and literature—and our talented authors, illustrators, designers and photographers have won many prestigious awards. We welcome you to explore the wealth of information available on Asia at **www.tuttlepublishing.com.**